In the Shadows of a Fallen Wall

In the Shadows
of a Fallen Wall

SANFORD TWEEDIE

University of Nebraska Press   Lincoln & London

Parts of this book originally appeared elsewhere. In chapter 1, the op-ed piece appeared as "Echoes of America: German School Siege Reflects U.S. Influence" in *The Philadelphia Inquirer* on April 30, 2002 (A13). Chapter 4, "Concrete Details," appeared in a slightly different form as "Erfurt: Your Guide's Tour" in *Exquisite Corpse* 10 (Fall 2001). Two pieces of flash fiction in Chapter 9, "The Class That Doesn't Exist in the Country That Once Did," appeared elsewhere: "American, the Beautiful" in *Doorknobs and BodyPaint* 49 (February 2008) and "The New Economy" under the title "Stimulus Package" in *Word Riot* (June 2009). Chapter 10, "Whatever You Do, Don't Look Down," originally appeared in slightly different form in *The Funnel, the Newsmagazine of the German-American Fulbright Commission* 37 no. 2 (Fall 2001). And in Chapter 11, "In Former Times," the excerpt by Roberta Harvey appeared in *The Funnel, the Newsmagazine of the German-American Fulbright Commission* 37 no. 1 (Spring 2001).

All photographs, including cover, by the author.

Library of Congress Cataloging-in-Publication Data
Tweedie, Sanford, 1962–
In the shadows of a fallen wall / Sanford Tweedie.
pages cm
Includes bibliographical references.
ISBN 978-0-8032-7141-8 (pbk.: alk. paper) 1. Tweedie, Sanford, 1962– 2. Authors, American—Biography.
3. Americans—Germany—Biography. 4. Berlin Wall, Berlin, Germany, 1961-1989—Biography. 5. Erfurt (Germany)—Biography. I. Title.
PS3620.W43Z46 2013
814'.6—dc23   [B]   2012045748

Set in Lyon Text by Laura Wellington.

For Callan, Tara, and Roberta,
for whom I would climb any wall

And for Manuela and Wilfried,
Thomas and Evy, and all their
children, who shared their lives
with us

The past is never quite past.
—TIMOTHY GARTON ASH

Nothing ever really disappears.
—LUTZ RATHENOW

Contents

Acknowledgments

As with any book, an author's name appears on the front, but the words within are created with the help and guidance of many others.

This book would not exist without the backing of three institutions: the Fulbright Commission, which granted me the award allowing me to teach in Germany for a year; the University of Erfurt, which gave me a home where I could do that teaching; and Rowan University, which has provided generous institutional support during the writing of this book.

In Erfurt, so many clerks, cashiers, *Strassenbahn* operators, wait staff, and others made up the majority of our daily encounters and formed our positive attitudes about people living in the city and the former East Germany. But I would especially like to recognize the kindness shown by the staffs of Albert-Schweitzer-Gymnasium and Haus der Bunte Träume (House of Colorful Dreams) Kindergarten, who welcomed and supported our children in ways we could not have imagined.

At University of Nebraska Press, many helped see this book through to publication. Heather Lundine, former editor in chief, helped me to restructure the book and supported the revised manuscript. Bridget Barry stepped in for Heather, providing patience and further guidance. Project editor Ann Baker and copyeditor Stephen Barnett helped to refine my words even more.

Several people also read earlier drafts and provided invaluable feedback. The late Denise Gess, novelist and teacher extraordinaire, read an early version of the book and encouraged me not to give up on it. Reviewer Julija Šukys understood my intentions and vision like no other. Manuela Linde toiled to make my German somewhat comprehensible. Finally, the feedback and ideas of my wife, Roberta Harvey, are infused in every word.

I shall admit my own weakness, at any rate; for I never bring
back home the same character that I took abroad with me.

—LUCIUS ANNAEUS SENECA

Introduction
The Walls in Our Heads

On the morning of April 26, 2002, my then five-year-old
daughter and I walked out the back door of our home, load-
ed down with her supplies for kindergarten and mine for
work. We made our way to the car parked in the driveway of
our home in a small southern New Jersey town. After strapping Callan into her seat, I started the engine and turned on
NPR as we waited for Roberta, my wife and Callan's mom,
to catch up. It was 8:00 a.m.

In his resonant voice and distinctive intonation, Carl Kasell led off the program: "Reports out of Germany say a school
shooting has left two dead." I knew—not suspected, knew
in a desperate desire not to—that when he went on to identify the location, it would be Erfurt, the city we had moved
from only eight months prior. Kasell continued: "Police in
Erfurt say that a gunman entered the Gutenberg Gymnasium shortly after eleven a.m. German time and began . . ."
11:00 a.m. in Germany; 5:00 a.m. our time. Three hours ago.
That almost-morning hour when most everyone is asleep. I
had been far into my night's slumber. Had I stirred? Rolled
over? Possibly.

As Kasell narrated the still-sketchy details about the
shooting—the fatality count would eventually rise to six-

teen—I began to better understand what it meant to have lived in the former German Democratic Republic for nearly a year and the impact our time on the other side of the now-drawn-back Iron Curtain had on our lives. My immediate reactions were captured in a piece I wrote that morning for the *Philadelphia Inquirer* op-ed page:

> When I heard the news about the shooting at Gutenberg School in Erfurt, Germany, my first concern was for our German friend's daughter who goes to high school in the city. My second thought was that it is now clear how much America's influence has pervaded the once-communist and Soviet-controlled German Democratic Republic.
>
> My first fear was soon alleviated. As soon as I reached work, I e-mailed my friend in Erfurt. She replied right away, assuring me that the incident had not taken place at her daughter's school and that her daughter was home safely.
>
> But my second fear did not disappear so quickly. Nor do I think it ever will. My family spent the 2000–2001 academic year living in Erfurt while I taught at the University, whose most famous student was Martin Luther. Erfurt is a beautiful, medieval town of two hundred thousand that was spared almost completely from World War II bombing. Resplendent with small community gardens and home to an international gardening center, Erfurt is known as the "garden city."
>
> My daughter Tara, who was then thirteen, attended one of the city's nine Gymnasiums, combination middle and high schools for the college bound. She loved it. The students were kind, caring, and non-cliquish. They embraced Tara as a friend, despite her barely being able to speak German when she arrived. Best of all, they were noncompetitive, enjoying one another's company. Such attitudes, we would come to learn, reflected those of the larger society. Far from the ste-

reotype of gruff, no-nonsense Germans, we found eastern Germans to be friendly, easy-going and fun-loving people.

Yet, the town and the area—indeed all of the former East Germany—are in transition from a communist to a free market society. This is represented by stark contrasts. For example, in the middle of our neighborhood of Soviet-designed, concrete apartment buildings, capable of housing some forty thousand people, squatted a recently built mall that looked for all the world like any mall found in the United States. Big Mercedes share the road with the remaining East German-era Trabants—small, fiberglass cars powered by little more than a lawnmower engine.

And though only a handful of Americans live in the town, America's influence is undeniable. Erfurt is home to McDonald's, Burger King, Pizza Hut, Woolworth's and Ford dealerships. Even in German stores, American logos are popular. American music fills the airwaves.

The contrasts are found in more than just the buildings and products; they are also found in the people—those who recall what eastern Germans refer to as "former times" and those who are too young to remember life under communism. Indeed, my university students, who tended to range in age from about twenty to twenty-three years, are the last of the generation who have any memory of living in the GDR. Their younger siblings were unable to recall the fall of the Berlin Wall.

I gave several talks on American youth culture to school teachers during my stay. To introduce the topic, I would ask two questions. The first was, "How much are teens here like teens in America?" The follow-up question was, "And how much do you want them to be like teens in America?"

Let me offer a story in response. While living in Erfurt, we awoke one morning to find that our car had been stolen.

It was recovered by police a few hours later. Riding with the police to the local garage where the car had been towed, I asked one of the officers whom he thought had committed the crime. "Dumme Jungs," he responded. Stupid boys. He then went on to say that the problem with kids today was a lack of leadership. What he meant was that since the fall of the Wall, there was no one keeping an eye on the kids; that the structured and busy lives forced upon people by the East German government were replaced by nothing; that kids had too much time to hang out, see what they didn't have and imagine the criminal means to get it. Clearly, he was lamenting that cradle-to-grave care and oversight provided by the GDR had disappeared, that "former times" were over.

Robert Steinhäuser, the nineteen-year-old gunman in Friday's shootings, proved that they are. He reportedly told a classmate, "One day, I want everyone to know my name and I want to be famous." He got his wish. He now becomes the poster child for the new eastern German, one whose memory does not include a time when the "e" in "east" was capitalized, one who has grown up with the conflicting tenets of Western values. More significantly, Steinhäuser's legacy results from his adoption of methods for coping with the system's pressures that we in the West are far too familiar with.

Dumme Jungs.

When an editor of the op-ed page tried to contact me to say he planned to run the piece, I was on my way home from work and, in my pre–cell phone days, missed his call. I didn't notice until later than evening his message on the home answering machine saying that I could see the proofs. By then I figured it was too late to do anything for the morning paper.

Even if I were given the chance to consider the editor's changes, I am not sure I would have argued too strongly against them. I don't think I would have said, "It's my way or don't publish it, Mr. Editor." While his changes and excisions tightened the piece without altering its tenor, in a move that I felt made the piece more inflammatory, he changed the beginning and ending. The published opening removed the first two paragraphs above and thrust to the front information I had included for my byline: "As a Fulbright scholar during the 2000–2001 school year, I lived in Erfurt, the eastern German city where 16 people were slain inside Gutenberg school Friday. When I heard the news, one of my first thoughts was that it is now clear how much America's influence has pervaded the once-communist former German Democratic Republic."

This not only removed my genuine concern for those whom I feared might have been harmed in the shooting, it also made me seem as if I were flouting my credentials. I had put them in the byline to explain why I had been in eastern Germany,[1] not to wave the award in the reader's face. The editor also altered the closing by cutting out the *Dumme Jungs* as the last sentence, thus removing my final condemnation of Steinhäuser, the young shooter who turned the gun on himself after being confronted by a teacher during his spree. Even the change in title from my "School Shooting Shows That East Germany Has Now Joined the West" to "Echoes of America: German School Siege Reflects U.S. Influence" shifted the agency of the relationship.

Still, when I saw the piece as it was published along with my e-mail address in the byline, I didn't anticipate the wrath that would follow. The morning of publication, I arrived at

1. Following the precedent set in the op-ed piece, I use the lowercase "e" in "east" and "eastern" to refer to the land formerly known as East Germany. The capitalized "East" and "East Germany" refers to that era when the German Democratic Republic existed.

work to my first e-mail response. It referred to my "inane screed," asserted that I was a professor because I wasn't "smart enough to get a real job," and called me a "loser" because "Never once have you mentioned something leftist/liberal pansies hate to talk about, 'personal responsibility'!!"

E-mails continued to arrive throughout the day. Later in the week, the editorial was reprinted in other newspapers, and a new wave of responses ensued. After my initial shock at the personal excoriations evolved into bemusement, I found that those who took the time to write offered two lines of counterargument. The first follows the logic of the letter above: *Your agenda, somehow related to a position in academia and obviously part of a larger, easily classifiable, liberal group-think, causes you to believe incorrectly that people are socially constructed, that they operate within and against societal norms and expectations, whereas in reality they have complete free will.* This, the letter writers go on to argue, causes me to blame American society and its influence, excusing the individual who should be held personally—and singularly—responsible for his actions. Taken to its extreme, the argument compares me to terrorists who also blame the United States for everything that is wrong with the world. "You and Bin laden [*sic*] are a pair. Everything is America's fault," one e-mail proclaimed. In a world but a few months removed from 9/11, such comparisons should not have surprised me.

Others, though somewhat less vitriolic, were uncanny in their resemblance to the first. One saw me as a "charter member of the 'Blame America First' society" and a "devotee of the 'It's Always Someone Else's Fault' cult." This writer went on to recommend that "you might consider returning to instruct those unfortunate victims, whom you have determined were better off under a failed Socialist experiment in East Germany, on the pitfalls of embracing a culture you have so ardently rejected." Another wrote that I had "absolutely no rational grounds for contending the nutcase shot up his school because his delicate psyche was bruised by American culture ... His actions might just as easily have been a product of child-rearing practices common to your own liberal, socio-ideological class."

These e-mailers are correct in saying that demonstrating direct causality between societal standards—be they east German or American—and a single person is impossible. In using the word "influence" in the opening paragraph where I discuss "how much America's influence has pervaded the once-communist and Soviet-controlled German Democratic Republic," I was suggesting in that overly simplified, brief editorial space that Robert Steinhäuser adopted a Western-style solution to his situation and that such an act indicates a shift in eastern Germans' perspectives that now align them with western perspectives. If anything, the e-mailers' free-will position supports my point. In his famous 1963 "Ich bin ein Berliner" speech outside Rathaus Schöneberg, President John Kennedy said of Berlin, "What is true of this city is true of Germany—real, lasting peace in Europe can never be assured as long as one German out of four is denied the elementary right of free men, and that is to make a free choice." The fall of the Wall provided Steinhäuser his ability to choose, even if he chose badly.

The logic of the second argument reasons: *Germans are Germans are Germans, and those who once massacred innocents in the world wars are fated to do it again. Robert Steinhäuser is just the latest incarnation of German evil.* Such an argument relies on a belief in cultural genetics, wherein an inherited predisposition, in this case toward evil, is passed down from generation to generation within a society. One correspondent stated, "Germany needs no lessons from anyone on how to kill innocent people." Another wrote that the country that "gave us two world wars and the holocaust hardly needs inspiration from us for violence." Yet another said, "The killer is the heir to the Nazi and Soviet cultures of mass murder." Finally, this one even uses a term similar to my "cultural genetics": "Since when do Germans need outside motivation to commit horrendous acts of violence . . . violence is just part of their cultural profile."

Even if cultural genetics—representing the nature side of this nature vs. nurture dichotomy—holds some credence, why should we see Steinhäuser, a nineteen-year-old who spent, at most, six years living under the communist regime, as a product of this society? Should it not be his elders—those with much more direct contact with communism and its behaviors—who go on shooting sprees? People's fundamental values were upended. Many remain conflicted by living in a capitalist marketplace after having been raised in a communist society. They don't understand how to be capitalists, whatever that might mean. And because some can't figure it out, or have and don't like what they see, or are too old to be successfully integrated into the free-market economy, there are people in eastern Germany who would prefer to see a return to GDR times. I have spoken with some of them, and their attitudes are reflected in the popularity of former communists in eastern German elections. And for those who lament what has taken place since *die Wende*—the "turning point" signifying the beginning of reunification—Steinhäuser's actions provide further evidence that "former times" were indeed better. See, they say, this massacre wouldn't have happened under the old system. It proves that the new system is unpredictable and dangerous.

While I might concede that either of these lines of reasoning—the personal responsibility or the cultural genetics argument—carries some validity, when taken together, they contradict one another. If Robert Steinhäuser's "cultural profile" as a German led him to go on the shooting spree, how can he—and only he—be personally responsible for this incident? If he is a manifestation of German culture, he cannot also be a youth willfully capable of accepting or rejecting societal influences. This also leads to questions about American society: If the violent German culture is so obviously reflected in this incident, what do the many more violent and super-violent crimes in the United States, in schools and in society at large, say about our own cultural genetics? And, perhaps more important, what, if anything, can be done about it if we are culturally predisposed to such violence?

Although both camps of e-mail correspondents reject any association between our country and the shooting, Germans themselves do not see it this way. A *Time* magazine article's title—"Germany's Columbine"—encapsulates the point of my op-ed piece in two words. In this piece, a German news anchor states, "It's the kind of thing you expect to happen in America." Echoing this, a German student points out, "This happens a lot in America, but it's not just an American thing anymore." Or as one student's mother succinctly puts it: "We've been Americanized." Having lived in German society—or at least on the fringe of it—I felt I could share my understanding and knowledge of this perspective in the *Inquirer* piece. Thus, I included the discussion from the police officer as representative of some east Germans' views. How ironic—and perhaps revealing of their biases—that many of those who e-mailed attributed those words to me.

The solution to this nature vs. nurture debate lies, not surprisingly, somewhere between the two dichotomies. To gain a more complete perspective, one should look at the situation not in terms of *either/or* but *both/and*. We need *both* to hold

Steinhäuser responsible for his actions *and* to acknowledge that society plays a role in such a crime. I see his actions as indicative of, not representative of, eastern Germany's situation. My editorial suggested that Steinhäuser's actions provide a demonstrable signal that the former East Germany has somehow turned a corner. Perhaps I would go so far to say that the shooting serves as an indicator that eastern Germans have bought into Western views.

And isn't this what we wanted when the Wall fell? We did not expect West Germans to adopt East German (that is, communist) values, but that West German culture would flow eastward. I do not claim that capitalism is inherently evil. I am not trying to defend the young man's cowardly actions. I am not arguing for a return to the GDR—the Stasi was certainly no Cub Scout troop. But to pretend that American values are, like people themselves, subject to a border check and can be forced to remain in the United States is naïve and isolationist. Would those who argue against America's sphere of influence extending beyond our borders also presume that the classics should not be studied, that the ideas found in Greek and British writings should be turned away at our borders? Would they postulate that terrorists' (re)actions are completely unrelated to the spread of American values and influence? The e-mailer who claimed, "You and Bin laden are a pair. Everything is America's fault" was at least partially correct. While I take umbrage at the inference, I do believe that the terrorist Osama bin Laden would not have existed without an America to direct his destructive anger toward, in the same way Moby Dick spurs Ahab's maniacal actions.

I will also forward another comparison that, were this an opinion piece, might inspire a new wave of e-mail rants: In their aggregate, the three dozen responses to my editorial point out how the Internet has created its own form of surveillance, one that echoes the East German Stasi. Those who publish in a digitally mediated world—either through corporate channels such as the *Philadelphia Inquirer* or through blogging and social networking—face a multitude of unknown and anonymous watchers who are only too eager to police and judge. Just look at the comments section following any controversial topic. Our perceptions of what we're willing to share have changed in an Internet world; our willingness to impose our perspectives on others has also shifted. And while the vast network of East German informants who spied on colleagues, friends, and even spouses may have reached one in five citizens at its zenith, these people had to be recruited by the Stasi; cybersociety encourages anyone and everyone to fulfill this role.

I was reassured that my perspective was not completely off base when I received an e-mail from my friend Manuela Linde, whose school-age daughter, Anne-Katrin, I initially worried about when I heard the news of the Erfurt shooting. Manuela wrote:

Almost one week after this tragedy happened, everybody here tries to find out reasons why. People do not talk about anything else—in town, on the tram, at work. Tomorrow is the public funeral service on Domplatz. People never have met there for a sad reason, at least since I have lived in Erfurt. I am quite sure that there will be more people than ever before, even more than on Dec 31, 1999. It certainly will be broadcasted all over the world.

Of course, there is not only one reason for why this could happen. The explanations go in three directions. First, how such a young boy could legally buy these lethal weapons (they already discuss to tighten up the German law). Second, that violence is present everywhere and every day on TV, in computer games, on the Internet. Third, Thuringia is the only German state in which pupils do not receive any kind of school leaving certificate if they fail the *Abitur*.[2] Due to this, the pressure of passing the *Abitur* is enormous.

Your article made clear how I have not heard anybody seeking the explanation about the non-existent future prospects of the young generation or the contrasts after the Wall came down. Perhaps it does not fit in the election campaign that has already started half a year before the elections. I do not know if the pupils in gymnasiums have already completely recognized their situation. It is the parents who either have too much work so that they do not have time for the problems of their children or they are unemployed and are so busy with their own problems that they do not listen to their children either. There was a survey among young people below age 25 last year. 70% said they will definitely leave Eastern Germany during the next years. About 15% were undecided and only 15% said they would stay. What a future!

It is good to hear your view on the things since you are an insider and outsider at once.

I found this last sentence heartening. For the year that I lived in Erfurt, I felt myself an outsider in the east. My inability to speak German well and my temporary status made me feel removed from society. Yet, we ventured to Erfurt for exactly that reason. My wife and I were somehow attract-

2. The German education system tracks students based on ability, starting in fifth grade. Graduates of a *Gymnasium* take the *Abitur* exam, which permits them to then study at German universities. When Steinhäuser was expelled from Gutenberg Gymnasium, he was left with no opportunity to obtain a degree. The Thuringian government has since rectified this situation.

ed to the idea of having all the rules that govern our daily lives—housing, food acquisition, transportation, and, most important, basic communication—yanked out from under us and then seeing how well we would function. And to do this in a society that had recently undergone a similar shift made it even more attractive. Of course, we had our safety net: employment while there, a house and jobs to return to. This made our risk-taking less adventuresome than it might have been, less realistic than it would have been for eastern Germans. But we still learned something during our stay, and not just about life in eastern Germany. While living there, and afterward as the discussion above shows, we became more aware of the matrix of cultural assumptions we Americans—like people in any society—operate within.

This was affirmed by the e-mails. In them, I saw a refusal to believe that anything American culture creates could have an impact elsewhere, despite U.S. television shows such as *Baywatch* and *Wheel of Fortune* being among the world's most syndicated; a refusal to consider that the Germany of today could be different from the Germany of the early and mid-twentieth century; and a refusal to imagine that people and circumstances change. In her September 5, 2002, "Give Class of 2006 a Chance to Create Its Own Syllabus," *Philadelphia Inquirer* editorialist Jane Eisner contends that such views result from "a fear of the unknown, a fear that the familiar will be replaced by the foreign—when, of course, true education is all about venturing into other, unsettling worlds, trying them on in your mind, and growing stronger for the effort."

I believe that those who e-mailed me about my editorial—and the dozens or even hundreds who only muttered under their breath or said something to the person across the breakfast table—found in me what in biology is called a "search image": an object of prey. While focusing on the search image may increase the likelihood for success, the predator must ignore other information in the landscape, reducing its competency for performing other tasks, often to its own detriment. This situation is illustrated in the depiction of a small fish about to be devoured by a larger fish, which is in turn about to be devoured by an even larger fish. When my editorial entered the letter writers' line of sight, I became their search image, the prey they had been seeking. Like my correspondents, I too am a predator focusing on my search image; unlike them, I will admit to my limitations.

1. Breaking Down the Wall

Because this book examines the importance of psychological, linguistic, and attitudinal walls, my hope was to begin by clearly and succinctly laying out the facts concerning the barricade that ran through Germany during communist rule in the German Democratic Republic. For those of us not from Germany, what the Wall represented symbolically was always more important than its actual function. As a physical manifestation of the Iron Curtain, the Wall conveniently fit the Cold War narrative. Its fall brought with it the collapse of the East German state, the return of a unified Germany, the end of communism in Europe, and the thawing of Cold War entrenchments. But like the small ball of mercury my ninth-grade biology teacher so naively let us roll around on the black lab bench, whenever I try to put my thumb on a definition of the Wall, it skitters away from me. The Wall itself—despite its symbolic concreteness—is not easily describable.

To begin, referring to the Wall in the singular is inaccurate. There was not really one wall but two—the Berlin Wall that encircled West Berlin and the one that ran between the two Germanys that had been divided since World War II's end. The Berlin Wall—the Wall—is the one people are most familiar with, the one that received so much media attention since first being erected in 1961, yet it was actually the last part of the Wall to be built. Between the end of World War II and 1952, Germans could freely travel between eastern and western portions of the divided country. In May of that year, concerned over the exodus of people—especially skilled workers—that has been estimated at close to three and half million in a country of eighteen million, the East German government acted to restrict the outward flow of citizens by constructing a fence along the inner border between East and West. Shaped like a very crooked "L," this wall eventually zigzagged from the Baltic Sea several hundred miles south before turning east and running to then-Czechoslovakia. In Berlin—an island within East Germany—the borders remained open, with some traffic restrictions, for nine more years. In August 1961, this border was closed without warning and the first concrete barricades installed a few days later.

In addition to the inaccuracy of referring to the two walls as a singular entity, to speak of the Wall as simply a wall is also incorrect. In reality, the Wall consisted of multiple components and, over the years, went through many iterations. Like the people it was meant to keep in and out, the Wall lived through several generations of change. When first constructed, the Wall was really nothing more than a barbed-wire fence. This was soon replaced with concrete barriers, which evolved into a fifteen-foot-high wall that blocked outsiders' ability to see—and get access to—what lay behind.

Eventually, this one wall also became two walls because the wall keeping people in ended up not being the same one keeping people out. A parallel set of walls were separated by a twenty-to-thirty-yard fortified obstacle course known as No Man's Land or the "death strip" because those who entered it would be shot without warning. Moving from East to West—as those who entered this forbidden zone were most likely to be doing—one would be confronted with some combination of the following impediment-ridden area, depending on the region of the country the Wall was located in: the hinterland fence, an electrified fence that set off an alarm when touched, anti-vehicle traps and trenches, a patrol strip, another strip filled with nail beds to blow out tires, observation towers, a strip of raked sand to detect incursions, a corridor with watchdogs, and tripwires attached to machine guns. The final barrier always consisted of the *Mauer feindwärts*, the "wall facing the enemy."

The view of the Wall from East and West also ended up being quite different. For those in the East, the Wall represented a bland cover to an intriguing book they would never be allowed to read, though they might catch glimpses of random pages—from news sources, sanctioned visits, relatives, rumors, or Western television signals. Even taking pictures of the Wall from the East German side was illegal. West Germans treated the Wall more as a coloring book on which to express themselves through art and graffiti. Because the GDR did not wish to seem overly aggressive in constructing the Wall, it was placed a few feet back from the actual border. For an artist standing near the western side of the *Mauer feindwärts*, each stroke became an act of defiance as he or she stood on East German soil, simultaneously defiling and beautifying their side of the *Mauer feindwärts*.

Similarly, the East and West German governments viewed this structure differently. The GDR maintained that the border between the Germanys was an international one, thus confirming, in their view, the German states' independence from one another. Officials referred to the Wall as the *antifaschistischer Schutzwall*, the "anti-fascist protective barrier." According to this moniker, the Wall helped East Germany keep marauding fascists from entering. West Germans preferred to see the border not as an international one, but as an internal or "inner German border." This term retained the perception that Germany was temporarily divided rather than being two separate countries, both of which happened to be populated by German speakers. The division extended to border crossers. The GDR viewed those leaving the country without permission as criminals, *Republikflüchtlinge*, "fugitives from the republic." West Germans saw such people as refugees of a despotic government.

These different perspectives necessitate an examination of the role and function of any wall. Normally a wall is a structure meant to keep elements, observers, and intruders from seeing or entering a particular area. It encloses and protects. While the East German walls functioned in this way, they did so not by walling out but by walling in. The Berlin Wall, in particular, did not simply divide the city in two, but enclosed West Berlin. It functioned, also counterintuitively, not so much to keep West Germans out of the East but to keep East Germans within the larger area outside the Wall. No one, we must remember, was shot running from West to East.

Such actions are important to consider, as well. The physical Wall's ability to keep anyone from entering or exiting the GDR was ultimately symbolic. With enough time, determination, and luck, most anyone could have gone over, under, or through the Wall. It was the guards—embodiments of the GDR state—who prevented this from occurring. It was the guards who stood between East German citizens and their attempts to cross the Wall. It was the guards who shot, on order, about 150 East Germans trying to escape to the West.

Ironically, in the early days of the Wall these same guards

were often the ones attempting to escape. The GDR adopted a deterrence strategy that involved indoctrinating guards into state ideology and, just as important, placing them in groups of two and three to keep watch on one another. These tactics—indoctrination and mutual observation—would come to define the GDR.

Robert Frost once contemplated, "Something there is that doesn't love a wall, / That wants it down." Yet the sentiment is often not enough to bring down a wall. In his 1963 "Ich bin ein Berliner" speech, President Kennedy said that the Wall was "dividing a people who wish to be joined together." Still, it wasn't until a quarter of a century later that the Wall's fall gave these people the opportunity to do so. And the reality of being joined can be painful to those who experience it. Though the physical Wall may have fallen years ago, mental ones remain. Germans speak of *die Mauer im Kopf*, the "wall in the head." Perhaps Kennedy was right that ideally those two people wanted to be one, but the reality of doing so has created a new inner German border.

Stereotypes persist, with the eastern Germans seeing western Germans as arrogant colonialists, while westerners complain of whiny and self-pitying easterners. A large majority of eastern Germans see themselves as neither part of their former country nor part of the combined country. Even today, only 22 percent of eastern Germans consider themselves "real citizens" of the reunified Germany, though that percentage grows to 40 for those under age twenty-five. Thus, when Lutz Rathenow says of reunification in *Ost-Berlin: Life Before the Wall Fell*, "Growing together takes time," one imagines that perhaps he left off "and the passing of those who refuse to accept change." Just as people once built, maintained, and patrolled the Wall, it remains people who retain these walls in their heads, disavowing the shift that many call progress. Some who lived it prefer to romanticize the country's history and their individual stories, relics from a time spoken of in the past tense but for them not yet past.

The demise of the Wall has necessitated a new kind of guard: one who not only witnesses (or has witnessed) but who also questions upon seeing, one whose trigger finger works a keyboard, a paintbrush, or a camera rather than a gun. During our stay, I ran across Brian Rose's *The Lost Border*. The book documents through photos his travels along the Iron Curtain beginning in the mid-1980s. In "Oebisfelde, East/West German Border, 1987" the photographer, who is not pictured, stands in a fallow field several hundred feet from the Wall, its collapse still unforeseen. Mottled by sunlight, the foreground consists of snow that is in places gray and in places brown but remains largely white. In the background, the stark light is unencumbered by cloud shadows.

Even the drifting snow appears afraid to approach East Germany. It stops a third of the way up the photo, replaced by parallel ruts of tillage moving away from the viewer. These lines would converge at the horizon if not for the thick concrete line dividing the middle of the photo. The top half of the photo reveals more gray, a sky as colorless as the area it rests above.

The small town of Oebisfelde squeezes between the Wall and sky. Tops of houses, church steeples, and barren trees peek over the Wall. A dark plume rises ominously from the middle of town. The smoke seems to begin at a church, as if it were on fire, and drifts low across the town, floating past a guard tower as it moves across the Wall, uninhibited, uninterrogated, a GDR gift to the West.

In my imagination, this picture was not taken by a photographer who parked his car and walked through the field, coming closer and closer to the Wall, knowing he was being observed by the East German guards and so making sure he kept a safe distance. Rather, I envision this from the perspective of someone who was, a few moments earlier, much closer to the Wall. The feeling is one of the viewer, a *Republikflüchtlinge* perhaps, taking one last look back over a shoulder as he scampers away from the area.

Maybe I imagine this perspective now because it fits my view of the world since leaving eastern Germany, my search image being limited by my experiences. More accurately, though, I believe that my year in the former GDR bears similarity to that moment when one emerges from a darkened interior into the sunlight. A brief period of near blindness ensues as pupils constrict against the light's overstimulation. The greater the contrast between light and darkness, the longer this adjustment takes. *In the Shadows of a Fallen Wall* captures some of those instances when I paused in the blinding light, waiting for my pupils—those light receptors that turn everything upside down before the brain rights it all again—to become more constricted and thus more receptive to seeing what was before me. This decreased field of vision increased my sphere of understanding. Trying to capture in words these witnessed images of my world turned upside down is no less complicated than trying to describe the Wall itself.

2. But for the Weather

Less than two weeks after Wilfried Linde turned three years old on August 4, 1961, GDR leader Erich Honecker ordered the construction of barbed wire and antitank obstacles to separate the two Berlins. When these were followed by concrete barriers, Wilfried's parents could—permit me the cliché—read the writing on the wall. The parents, strong believers in *Kapitalismus*, quickly reached a decision. In October, the couple and their young son traveled to Berlin, supposedly to visit friends. The plan involved waiting until nightfall, strapping Wilfried to his father's back, then swimming across a channel of the River Spree under cover of fog. The escape would eventually lead to Toronto, where a factory foreman position already awaited Herr Linde.

As high school seniors in 1980, a friend of mine and I decided to spend the weekend in Toronto, a four-hour drive from our Michigan hometown on the Canadian border. That Friday morning, a winter holiday, we awoke to a snowstorm. But we were young and immortal, and began to drive. We crossed into Canada at the Blue Water Bridge, an international border I grew up within a mile of. We pushed through the blizzard, our travel time stretching to six hours. Arriving safely in Toronto, we headed straight to the Sheraton Centre, a hotel beyond our busboy-bankrolled means but known to me because I had once stayed there with my parents. Since the weather had forced so many people to cancel their reservations, we were quoted a rate half the normal price. This we could afford. We spent the rest of the afternoon in an indoor-outdoor pool. A plastic curtain hung into the water, dividing the two parts. Inside, chlorine filled our noses. Outside, we marveled at the forty-three-story concrete hotel rising into the sky as plump, wet snowflakes fell onto our faces.

My friend and I ate our first meal at a nearby restaurant, the Old Spaghetti Factory. We struck up a conversation with the locals at the table next to ours, bragging about driving to Toronto in the blizzard that had now dissipated outside. One of the young men, bearded and bearlike, laughed at our story and told us how, when he was a child, his family had escaped from East Germany by crossing a river in the fog. "Now *that*," he said, "is a triumph over the weather worth laying claim to."

In actuality, this conversation never took place. Because of the weather, seating was abundant and the table next to us that evening was empty.

And it was because of the weather that the Lindes never reached Canada. That first night in East Berlin, young Wilfried had been given a sleeping pill so he would not cry out or make any noise during the crossing. The family waited through a clear night. They spent much of the next day trying to get some sleep at the home of acquaintances. The second night, another pill for Wilfried, but again clear skies. The third night, the same. And the fourth. After a week, the family gave up.

Had there been any fog, Wilfried might have become one of those escapees to the West one can read about in books, the kind of person you might meet eating at the table next to yours. Had the family been caught, they most likely would have been imprisoned for a few years, after which Wilfried would have been treated as a pariah in school, the system sanctioning against those who tried to outwit it. Or they might even have become three early additions to the list of East Germans who died trying to escape. Had fog ever meandered in during those long nights, Wilfried Linde would not have grown up as he did.

Instead, the family returned to the Erfurt home they thought they would never see again and lived as citizens of the German Democratic Republic. Wilfried's father learned to prosper as a capitalist after all, opening his own automobile brake repair shop, eventually employing ten people and bringing in a million DDR marks per year. Even the communist leadership of East Germany understood the need for entrepreneurship in some service-oriented businesses and so allowed small, family-run firms, such as repair shops and restaurants, to exist for the profit of those involved. And Wilfried, the son, would later be employed as the factory foreman his father had planned on becoming in Toronto, albeit within the communist system.

Half a century after the uneventful trip to Berlin that changed the family's destiny, Wilfried's parents are both dead. Wilfried remembers nothing of the escape attempt; his parents did not even tell him about it until he was a teenager. There is no one who can bear witness to this past, this act of defiance that may, since the fall of the Wall, be shared willingly with friends and acquaintances but in former times had to remain a secret whispered only among family members and the very closest of friends.

Three of my earliest television memories are of viewing seminal national events: the first moon landing, the Vietnam War, and the Watergate hearings. While the moon landing produced the sort of cheering and hoopla normally afforded a Super Bowl, the latter two unfolded slowly on the screen, the line between news and soap opera blurring. I was too young to understand the intricacies of these situations and the players' roles. Nor can I say how these affected me directly. But they might have something to do with my general distrust in politicians despite always voting, a dislike of wars and suspicion of the motives behind them, and an unwavering belief that the short-lived Major Matt Mason spaceman action figure was much cooler than anything G.I. Joe—even with Kung Fu grip—could offer.

East Germany was not a childhood event, but rather an empty space perched on Walter Cronkite's shoulder, a slash of black separating East from West. Had Wilfried's family escaped and had I somehow met him in Toronto, I might have learned something about East Germany, something more than what I knew then. Which was basically nothing. It was as if a roof had been built atop the Wall that circumscribed the GDR's borders. My knowledge of the country derived from Cold War rhetoric. West Germans were our friends; East Germans, the enemy. And the roots of communist East Germany, I somehow decided or was led to believe, were traceable to Nazism. I have since learned that in East Germany, schoolbook history taught that West Germans were the direct descendants of Nazism and that when the government referred to "our friends," it meant the Soviet Union.

While my understanding of these situations has since been complicated, I am certain now that Wilfried Linde is my friend. Wilfried speaks little English and my German is deplorable, but we drink beer and grill bratwurst together. I laugh at the jokes he loves to tell—most of them *are* funny—and no matter what happens, he always reassures, "It's no problem." Roberta and I entrusted Tara to Wilfried and his wife, Manuela, while Tara spent a year as a high-school exchange student, and Wilfried and Manuela have done the same with their daughter, Anne-Katrin, when she studied in the United States. We have traveled from there to visit the Lindes; they have traveled here to visit us. Even though Wilfried and I rarely talk to one another and most correspondence is carried on via Manuela, we are certain—without ironic winking—who are friends are.

Prior to moving to the former East Germany, I never could have imagined that we would meet Wilfried, Manuela, and their children, let alone that our personal histories would end up so intertwined. Yet the unimagined becomes events experienced, then remembered. Each shift occasions, as do all personal histories, a telling and a retelling of the stories that are our lives.

I first visited the former GDR in 1992, a tourist who knew no one but his traveling companion, both of us Americans on extended stays in western Germany. I was teaching in Giessen, a small city north of Frankfurt within an hour's drive of the former border. I had stumbled onto a teaching exchange program between the University of Wisconsin-Milwaukee, where I was finishing my graduate coursework, and Justus-Liebig-Universität in Giessen. While an incredible learning experience, these were also two of the most cheerless years of my life: a long-term relationship was over but somehow would not end; I was caught in a career and social netherland, wedged between students who kept their deferential distance from instructional staff and professors who likewise kept their hierarchical distance; I knew little of the language and found few opportunities to learn it as my time not spent on teaching was dedicated to attempting to write a dissertation from afar; and, in the middle of all this, my father died, leaving me grieving a continent away from my family.

Naively, I had thought that since I had missed the actual event of the Wall coming down, there was not much to see in the land beyond where the Wall once stood. I heard the reports about all the money being poured into the east and surmised that it had been transformed overnight into a westernized state. Besides, with so much of Europe to visit, I didn't feel the need to spend my free time in another version of Germany.

But a few months before my two-year stay ended, Jim Soderholm, an American professor also teaching in Giessen, suggested that we should spend some time in the east. He wanted to see where his heroes—Bach, Goethe, and Schiller, the triumvirate associated with the Thuringian area—had lived as much as he wanted to see the former German Democratic Republic. He even offered to rent a car and drive us there.

Jim and I bounced across the southern portion of the former East in our nondescript white Volkswagen, determined to visit as many cities—Jena, Halle, Leipzig, Erfurt—and villages as we could in our week of travel. By the end, we had seen enough. I have a photo of Jim standing before a church with his hands on hips. It's not difficult to read his expression as he declares, "I refuse to cross the street to see another fucking church!" Without people to tell us their stories of these places, we were little more than water striders skittering across the surface of the east.

Though I was certain I had seen enough of eastern Germany on that trip, eight years later I found myself not only back in the east but living there and again teaching at a German university. I wondered how I had ended up repeating myself. Roberta and I had met the week after I returned from the Giessen teaching position in 1992 and were married two years later. Stepdaughter Tara was nine when Callan was born a few years after that. By the turn of the century, I had been at Rowan University long enough to apply for a sabbatical. I did not even consider Germany when first examining Fulbright opportunities, but the rest of the world offered nothing that seemed even remotely close to the sorts of things I profess to have some knowledge of. Indeed, the year I was looking, I could not find a single position that mentioned writing teachers. Frustrated, I turned to Germany. And there it was: "Newly reshaped country seeks short-term relationship with academic who can teach writing, culture and literature. Must be willing to relocate to former East." It was not without some trepidation of being selected that I responded to the ad. My anxiety grew when I was told I was chosen for the blind date. Still, Roberta's mother was born and raised in Augsburg, Germany, until her archetypal marriage to an American soldier, so Roberta was interested in the opportunity to experience her mother's homeland for an extended period, and I felt—based on my visit with Jim—the east would be different enough from the west to provide us interesting cultural and linguistic challenges. We decided to take a chance on the city I once thought I had thoroughly traversed in a couple hours.

In the fully furnished, former East German apartment that my family sublet from October 2000 to August 2001 were two shrines to technological advancement. One consisted of a computer workstation complete with a then state-of-the-art modem, CD-ROM drive, and printer. A few feet away a 19-inch TV with cable supported one of the apartment's three VCRs. Perhaps the placement was intentionally ironic, but atop this electronic foundation stood a trilogy of miniature communist-era books. Each was less than two inches high by one inch long and perhaps three-quarters of an inch thick, wide enough for the three to stand together without support.

The burgundy cover of the middle book read *Das Kapital*, Marx's manifesto that served as the theoretical underpinnings for the communist state. While Marx himself may have had difficulty recognizing his philosophy as exemplified by the GDR, we who shared the apartment with this tiny *Das Kapital* and its two comrades also had problems recognizing its function a decade after the end of communist rule. The books appeared to have been printed by the GDR government and were, I assumed by their size, meant to be carried everywhere and read at any time—on the bus, while waiting in line for food, at party rallies.

Or perhaps they were not read at all. Certainly, the print inside was smaller than I was able to decipher. It is possible that these books served only to display communist affiliation, brought forth from pockets and bags and held up as symbols of party devotion. Since people would understand both the absurdity and necessity of this action, I picture both adherents and nonadherents holding before them a book with print too small to read, a talisman to ward off attacks. In an era when one could often not be sure who spied for the government and who didn't—knowing only that many did—it was safer to behave like the others. Actions can be observed; thoughts cannot.

Indeed, one can often only guess at the role such GDR artifacts play in twenty-first-century Germany. Many GDR products are still popular today, including sparkling wines, schnapps, and candies, among others. These could represent nostalgia for that era. The term *Ostalgie,* which combines the German words for "east" and "nostalgia," was coined to describe this. Perhaps they serve as a reminder not to forget and thus repeat history. Or perhaps they poke fun at what has become the kitschiness of that era. Whatever the case, these remnants of East German life serve as souvenirs from a trip taken long ago. They give tangibility to the stories people tell.

For those of us who were not there and cannot look at East Germany as it existed before, such souvenirs provide a furtive, sidelong glance into this past. Like monuments and statues created by a state, such artifacts carry in their materiality the solidity we seek in our pasts rather than the uncertainty promised by futures not yet lived.

We spent the first six weeks of our year abroad in language-intensive instruction in Regensburg, in the former West, with other Fulbrighters. While there, the group took a weekend trip to Weimar, named a European City of Culture because of its rich history as home to many famous Germans, including Martin Luther, Franz Liszt, Richard Wagner, Richard Strauss, and Friedrich Nietzsche, in addition to Bach, Goethe, and Schiller. But Weimar also has a political history, providing the eponymous name for the Weimar Republic, which existed between the world wars, because the Republic's National Assembly created its constitution in the town. It also played host to the first national congress of the nascent Nazi Party. In Germany, such historical ironies are like Poe's purloined letter: They exist right before our eyes but remain unseen when we don't know the histories that accompany them. Political writer Timothy Garton Ash refers to this "intimate proximity of high European culture and systematic inhumanity." For Garton Ash, this is exemplified by the oak under which Goethe supposedly created his famous "Wanderer's Night Song" later becoming fenced in by Buchenwald, "the highest and the lowest in human history, together in one place."

Prior to reading Ash's *The File*, I discovered my own version of the Goethe Oak. As part of our Weimar tour, we were shown the Hotel Elephant, which sits on Marktplatz. Part of Thomas Mann's *Lotte in Weimar* takes place here. On a balcony stands a life-sized statue of Bach. He looks out regally over the square. During another part of the tour, we visited the nearby Buchenwald concentration camp. A scene in an introductory video shows Hitler espousing his brand of hatred to the crowd below. Clearly, he—not Bach—stands on the balcony of the Hotel Elephant.

Reflective of Weimar's preferred persona of embodying the best in German culture are the souvenirs available to tourists. Most of the gift shops and street vendors sell small, white, faux-marble busts of famous Germans. Roberta wanted one of Karl Marx, a droll nod to her referencing Marx in the dissertation she would finish writing in the land that was once home to "real existing socialism."

Roberta was sure she had seen a bust of Marx while we touristed about the town, but as we hurried back to our bus in the late afternoon she couldn't find it again. I reminded her that we would soon be moving to Erfurt, the next town over, and that we already had enough luggage to drag around. I convinced her to wait until we returned to make her purchase.

It took us several months to get back to Weimar, but Roberta's determination was resolute. During a Christmastime visit, she scoured the shops for the bust of Marx. Each seemed to carry the same line of heads: Liszt, Bach, Goethe, Schiller, and a choir of others who had no connection to Weimar but whose likenesses were offered up for those tourists who had missed their opportunities to purchase them elsewhere or who would not even make it to these other places.

Karl Marx was nowhere to be found. I began waiting outside as Roberta popped in and out of the shops.

"Just ask," I finally encouraged.

Roberta is often reluctant to do this in U.S. stores and was even more so in Germany, where only a few months into our stay she was still not confident in her nascent language abilities.

"Just ask," I repeated, as she came out of another store empty handed.

Snowflakes began floating from the sky and settling onto the head and shoulders of passers-by. On the ground, they melted, leaving only damp pavement.

Roberta emerged from the next store with her mouth open. She relayed that she had finally gathered the courage to inquire. The clerk responded with haughty disdain: "Wir haben keinen Karl Marx, und wir haben keinen Hitler." We have no Karl Marx, and we have no Hitler.

"Did you ask her if she would have said the same thing before the Wall fell?" I shot back.

Roberta hadn't. The irony would have been too much. The tourists' desire to take home a souvenir, an artifact, some sort of proof of having been in Weimar provides this store its reason for being, yet it also allows the clerk the opportunity to sit behind the counter and smugly declare to an American that the history she searches for—the one involving the once revered—no longer exists. The conquered has learned her lesson well: one must buy from those stores—and buy into those stories—that are available.

Still, I am sure that somewhere in eastern Germany on someone's mantel or end table, or even atop a VCR, a wan

Karl Marx casts doleful glances at the world around him. His vision filled with fog and rivers and lives altered by the weather, he understands that we amble along naively, often not noticing that history-altering events hold hands with the happenstance of our lives. Whatever the story, his eyes, forever watchful, remain empty.

In spring, often the feeling of being in another city.
One that smells of curiosity and new departures.
—LUTZ RATHENOW

3. Leaving the American Sector

At the end of a session during the 2000 Fulbright Orientation, we participants were given coffee mugs with *Das Neue
Berlin*—The New Berlin—printed on them. Silhouettes
of the city's recognizable structures wrap around the outside; just as many silhouettes of cranes are liberally placed
among them. Berlin was described to us as *eine Stadt im
Aufbruch*—a city facing a new departure. In this reunited
metropolis, where seemingly every building and road was
under renovation, the slogan fit. The resituated seat of the
federal government had been so transformed as to be sometimes unrecognizable to someone like myself who first visited just a few years after the Wall fell. Especially disconcerting was how the once-barren no-man's land of Potsdamer
Platz had, phoenix-like, arisen into a stunning array of ar-
chitecture housing Sony, DaimlerChrysler, a Grand Hyatt
Hotel, and an IMAX theater, among others.

For my family and me—and all the other Fulbrighters attending the conference who were not assigned to remain
in the city—Berlin's *eine Stadt im Aufbruch* nickname was
even more appropriate. For most of the twentieth century's
second half, Berlin was an island surrounded by communist Germany. Now it would serve as a Fulbright Ellis Island

for Americans who had emigrated from points throughout the United States, spent six weeks traveling through language lessons, and had now amassed here. This was our point of new departure before we were to spread out across the country. We were filled with the excitement of the new and the apprehension that we were to be banished from Berlin, the Fulbright organization a mother cat who abruptly decides her kittens have suckled long enough and must be weaned from her comforting milk.

I had not realized, until these orientation briefings, that the Fulbright organization carried with it an enormously politicized history. Prior to World War II, private organizations sponsored educational exchanges. As part of America's expanded role in global politics following the war, the government increased its involvement in these exchanges through the Fulbright and Smith-Mundt Acts, passed in 1946 and 1948, respectively. However, the "exchange" that accompanied these was unidirectional. In 1950, the U.S. government launched a "Campaign of Truth" which, as a means to combat communism, required exchange educators to propagandize American democratic values. Ideally, host countries absorbed and adopted these values, a not-so-furtive attempt at cultural imperialism. Yet some feared the reverse. The Fulbright organization had to fend off attacks from the likes of Joseph McCarthy and his allegations that the program officially sanctioned communist and other foreign spies' infiltration of the United States.

One session during our three-day orientation featured a trio representing the American Embassy. Though the attaché requested we be on our best behavior as emissaries of the United States, we were not told that we were responsible for indoctrinating Germans into the American way of thinking. Why should we? "Reunification" has meant the imposition of West German values on the East Germans. The West German constitution was adopted wholesale as the supreme law of the land, the eastern version apparently having nothing worthwhile to offer, and the West German social market economy replaced East German communism. Horst Kasner—father of Angela Merkel, reunited Germany's first Eastern-raised chancellor, and himself one of the few to move from West to East when as a pastor committed to resistance he transplanted his young family to an area in rural Brandenburg—contends: "I wanted a democratic East Germany. But the people wanted the deutsche mark. The revolution is now over." The victor in Germany is clear. There was no reason for us Fulbrighters to rub it in.

The night before we boarded a train to Erfurt, located more than three hours southwest of Berlin, I got up from my hotel bed fifteen stories above Alexanderplatz, an important transportation hub and gathering spot for East Berlin. I wandered over to the window where I paused to watch the red lights of the Fernsehturm, a TV tower. Built by East Germany in the 1960s, the tower was meant to be seen from anywhere in either Berlin and was viewed as a symbol of the power of the GDR. It remains the second-largest structure in Europe.

As I watched the lights blink silently and assuredly, I was reminded of the green light of Daisy's East Egg dock in *The Great Gatsby*. In my return to Germany, was I similar to Gatsby, who Nick observes reaching out for the green light in hopes of resurrecting a vanished past with Daisy? Was I trying to recreate my own painful German experiences from the early 1990s, to write over them with this new endeavor? Was my life a traffic light where I was the amber bulb currently caught between the red light of once-communist Erfurt and the green light of American capitalism? The teacher in me assigned myself a C- for thematic triteness and sentimentalism.

I continued watching the lights, nonmetaphorically this time. While I wasn't sure what I wanted or expected of eastern Germany, others tried to sway my opinion. The March prior, spring had arrived in south Jersey. The tiny, initial foray of snowdrops had been replaced by the daffodils and forsythias blooming their bright yellow. Tulips sprouted from the ground, though most had yet to flower. My freshmen composition students and I were beyond the stage of initial bloom. We had been together since January, and we had conferenced individually many times, so we were comfortable talking with one another about academic as well as personal issues. One morning, I informed the class of our plans to live in the former East Germany for a year. They were dumbstruck.

"Are you taking your kids with you?" one asked, incredulous.

"Your wife *wants* to go?" another demanded more than asked.

"Aren't you being selfish?" chimed in a third.

I laughed this off as belying the students' age and the provincialism I find common in this area despite being across the river from Philadelphia and only a couple hours' drive from New York, Baltimore, and the nation's capital. But my mother-in-law is not so blinkered. She was born and raised in Augsburg, Germany, and lived through nights of World War II air raids. During one, a bomb coming in on an angle ripped through their row house's third-floor bedroom—my mother-in-law, Karin's—then passed through the second floor of the house next door and landed in the third, killing the family hiding in the basement. Karin's family, having taken cover in their own basement, was unharmed. A year in Germany would give Roberta—her daughter and my wife—the chance to see her *Oma*, the grandmother who still lived in the same house in Augsburg, for the first time in twenty-five years. And Oma would get to meet Tara and Callan, her great-grandchildren, for the first time. Germany was also home to Karin's two brothers, their wives, a daughter, and even a long-lost German family from my father-in-law's side, whom he had been corresponding with for a decade. Yet, Karin seemed cool to the idea of our going. Perhaps it was her guilt at having been back to Germany only twice since she emigrated to marry the American serviceman she met at an Oktoberfest she was attending with her mother, a man who had drunk so much that he couldn't remember her first name when he picked her up for their initial date. Fortunately, he had written down her address, or two generations of children would not now exist. Perhaps she felt her daughter was backtracking in her footsteps, or that she did not want to relive the pain she must have put her own mother through. Whatever the reason, Karin showed little enthusiasm toward the opportunity.

Most disconcerting, though, was the comment from a

friend, a German scholar who has spent much time in that country. When I told him where I would be living for the next year, he replied that Erfurt was "the nicest city . . . in east Germany." The pause implied that the worst city in the west is nicer than any city in the east, but if we had to be stuck in the former GDR, Erfurt got his recommendation.

I finally turned from the window and moved to the bathroom. The bottoms of my feet began to vibrate against the cool tiles as the U-Bahn rumbled along more than fifteen stories below. I was reminded of another book, *The Quiet Assassin*, an East German spy novel in which the subway plays a crucial role. The two halves of the divided city interlocked like puzzle pieces, a tab in East Berlin notching into West Berlin. After the Wall went up, East Germany allowed three West Berlin subway lines to continue to pass under the East as they crossed this area, though no stops were made. This resulted in several *Geisterbahnhöfe*, subway stations that had been built prior to the Wall but became ghost stations that no longer functioned. In this Thomas Kirkwood novel, several members of a resistance movement attempt to escape to the West by first digging a tunnel to the subway platform. They jump into a passing subway whose car doors open as it moves slowly through the Stadion der Weltjugend station, thanks to an operative conductor. This being a spy thriller, the escape does not go according to plan.

Though there would be no failed escape attempts or double-crosses in our lives, all would not go according to plan, as we too would travel from west to east before reemerging in the west, albeit ten months later. Tomorrow, we would trade this reassuring position high above Alexanderplatz for the requisite complications that become our lives. And East Germany would reveal itself as a *Geisterbahnhof*, a deserted platform viewed only in a faded yellow glow while passing through. Because we can never stop in this once-existent land, I struggle to make sense of those artifacts of the East that are only glimpsed as time moves us away from them. In *After the Wall: Confessions from an East German Childhood and the Life that Came Next*, Jana Hensel points out this is true both for outsiders and for those who grew up in the East: "The GDR will recede into the distance, becoming ever smaller and more unreal, like an object in a car's rear-view mirror."

The train ride to Erfurt, located near the geographical center of the reunified country, began at Ostbahnhof, the main station in the former East German capital. As with so much from that era, this version of the Ostbahnhof has since been torn down and replaced. Under the glass and metal arch, the platforms were sparsely occupied. The people stood apart from one another, alone in their contemplation. They moved slowly, lethargically even, despite the sunshine after a day of rain. As they stared down the tracks not really searching for but resigned to the reality of the train that would take them away, we grew quiet alongside our fellow travelers.

Once aboard, we traveled quickly through the construction cranes to the western terminal, Zoological Garten. Only in comparison did we realize the grayness of the Ostbahnhof. The Zoo platform swarmed with people. The crowd, though paused in its travels, still moved to and fro, determined to get somewhere. Many chatted among themselves. The hum from these people was audible in the lull between the train noises. A man sat on a bench facing our train. Dressed in a suit and overcoat, he typed on a laptop computer. He stopped, pulled out what was then a still-uncommon cell phone, and placed it to his ear.

While the stations themselves contrasted sharply as we

traveled from Ostbahnhof to Zoo, it had not been clear when we had crossed that divide that was once the Wall. A wide swath of empty land had once ribboned through the city. The border, a manmade structure to begin with, had been replaced by manmade structures of a different sort. The vacuum that a city so abhors had been filled with stores and housing. We could not tell where life had repopulated the former death strip.

Had we walked through these streets, we might have been more easily able to identify where East became West. In addition to a line of bricks demarcating where the Wall stood, the casual observer can distinguish East Berlin from West Berlin by the pedestrian walk signals called *Ampelmännchen*. In the West, the red *wait* logo is a figure with arms pointing downward in the stance of a robotic cowboy about to draw both six-shooters during a gunfight. The *wait* signal in the East is more rounded and stylized. In contrast to the robotic figure, he seems whimsical. He wears a brimmed, flat-topped hat, arms extended at ninety-de-

gree angles from his body. And while the East and West *Ampelmännchen* are similar—a figure striding, arms akimbo—again the green figure from the East is more exaggerated in his movements. He is, ironically perhaps, moving forward, confidently progressing, strutting even. This token of a time past had set off an uproar from former Easterners when the government proposed to change all signals into the Western version. In an act of political wisdom, the authorities relented and retained this harmless remnant of the communist state.

The Checkpoint Charlie Museum, one of the most fascinating stops in Berlin, provides a more formal remembrance of the former border. Much of this storefront museum is taken up with exhibits on East Germans' attempts to escape to the West. Called "Desire is the Mother of Invention," the main exhibit showcases all sorts of escape methods involving going over, under or through the Wall: vehicles modified to hide someone, including within seats; homemade planes, hot air balloons, boats, and scuba equipment; tunnels that were filled in soon after they were constructed and follow-

YOU ARE LEAVING
THE AMERICAN SECTOR
ВЫ ВЫЕЗЖАЕТЕ ИЗ
АМЕРИКАНСКОГО СЕКТОРА
VOUS SORTEZ
DU SECTEUR AMÉRICAIN
SIE VERLASSEN DEN AMERIKANISCHEN SEKTOR
US ARMY

ing the escape of only a few or a few dozen people; even a suitcase carried by pedestrians into which a woman folded herself up as part of her successful attempt to go unnoticed. Such a positioning was metaphorically common in everyday life in East Germany, where surveillance was prevalent. Under such circumstances, many people tried curling up into the size of nothing to go unobserved.

After World War II, the Allies divided Berlin into four areas, each controlled by a different country: England, the United States, France, and Russia. Thus, at Checkpoint Charlie—the most famous of the border crossings around the city—a large white sign with black lettering informed travelers "You are leaving the American sector" in the three languages of the occupiers and in German. An original sign is housed in the Checkpoint Charlie museum along with a broken piece of actual pavement, the border painted directly onto the asphalt. A person can stand above the line, one foot in each of the Germanys.

Our escape from the west—without walls to cross and no guards to watch us—was less adrenalin filled and much less risky than those escapes from the East on display at Checkpoint Charlie. Yet pulling away from Berlin in the clacking train cabin filled with my family and our few pieces of luggage, I did not imagine how challenging and difficult such a straddling of borders could be.

We quickly left behind the noisiness of Berlin. Our first stop beyond the city limits was Dessau, in the former East. The clouds covered the sun, as if on command, graying everything. The buildings, the roads, even the trees appeared leaden and flat. Depth had disappeared. The platform reflected this grayness. The train screeched to a halt among tracks with weeds growing between the ties. The edges of the platform were crumbling. Three colorless figures waited to board, then did so mechanically, heads down.

The scene outside the window dismayed me. This weather seemed to linger over the east; the lack of color pervaded it. I worried that this drabness might infiltrate our mindset. The last few days in Berlin had been filled with excited conversation about finally moving to our new homes. Even our anxiety over the unknown was tempered by the thrill of the new. Now, the four of us slipped into silence, the rhythm of the train wheels marking our movement away from the west.

Farther down the metallic brown rails, the train slowed outside Bitterfeld. In the foreground loomed an elephantine corpse of a factory, its broken windows eye sockets plucked empty. The section closest to us had begun to decompose, whole walls of bricks falling away. Nearer still, hundreds of rusting hopper cars stood abandoned along spurs. I let out my breath as our train did not swerve onto the sidetracks to halt behind these. Instead, we continued on to Bitterfeld. The name "bitter field" is understandable. Seven construction workers displayed the only sign of color. Four, who rest-

ed near the end of the platform under renovation, wore fluorescent green work vests. Three others in orange vests stood
near large construction equipment at the opposite end.

On our way again, we saw a line of automobiles waiting—for how long?—at a light near the tracks. These came
in colors: blue, black, purple, red, yellow and green. It is easier to replace the cars than the buildings, which remained a
colorless brown.

Another station and, except for the cigarette advertisements, another gray platform. A barefoot man dressed in a
sleeveless black T-shirt and black shorts stood at the end of
the platform facing the same direction the train was headed. He juggled yellow, blue, and orange balls. But as soon
as we left him behind and moved further into the east,
we passed more fallow-brown buildings. The graffiti on
them—ubiquitous along walls facing the tracks—was painted in whites, blacks, and grays. Even the youth, any western
society's counterculturalists, had not found an alternative
to the monochrome of communism.

On the outskirts of Merseburg, another brick ruin of a factory. It was impossible to tell whether this one was in the pro-

cess of being torn down, was simply collapsing under its own weight, or had remained in this state since being bombed during World War II. Each explanation seemed equally plausible.

More towns. More stops. In Grosskorbetha, finally some color. Here the buildings were painted in pinks, yellows, and whites; one was even mauve. But these were pastels, washed-out colors. In Weissfels, different hues: blues and oranges. The landscape began to change from flatness to rolling hills, with the occasional farmhouse picturesquely situated atop a green fold of earth. Outside Naumburg, we passed a *Schrebergartenanlage*, a small community of gardens and weekend cottages. Two couples sat around a white plastic table drinking beer. They tilted their heads back and laughed as we rolled by.

The next town added green and gold to a palate of yellows, oranges, and the occasional peach. But in the middle of this hunkered yet another factory corpse. As the train trundled through the hills again, the trees unfolded, their leaves browns, golds, yellows. It was autumn, after all. The hues of death were majestic. These trees would, after the barren winter, bud the green of new leaves next spring. A town lay in the distance, its red-tiled roofs and white buildings checkerboarding the landscape. I closed my eyes and tried to rest, but sleep would not come.

When I opened them, we were outside Weimar, non-home to Karl Marx busts. I waited as we stopped at the station, then waited some more as we pulled away. Anxious, I looked out the window. Our next stop was Erfurt, but first we had to pass an unwatching sentry. A few minutes later, it appeared atop a hill, square against the sky. The Buchenwald Monument bell tower did not start small and grow larger as we neared but simply materialized. Erected by the Soviets after World War II, it memorializes antifascist (and largely communist) resistance fighters who were imprisoned by the Nazis and died inside the camp. As if these deaths deserved more recognition than those of the others who perished within. The monument serves as a reminder of how close trains carrying travelers from town to town passed the death within the woods. And of how trains making their way to Buchenwald, cars filled with prisoners, used these same tracks.

I wanted to curl into myself, but there was no one to carry me away from this except the train, whose wheels beneath the car clattered like teeth as we passed.

Within minutes, we were on the outskirts of Erfurt. We bisected large stores and smaller shops on both sides, auto dealerships filled with new cars, an Ikea warehouse. As we rolled into town, I leaned out the window. Wind whipped my face, the town slapping me with newness, promise, and the colors of advertising. The aroma of capitalism filled my nose again. Erfurt was different from anything we had seen on the train ride. Perhaps my German-scholar friend was correct.

The city's rich history dates back more than 1,250 years to 742, when St. Boniface established a church here and used it as his base from which to convert heathens to Christianity, although the city was probably founded even earlier. In medieval times, Erfurt served as a crossing point for two major European trade routes. The city monopolized the market for woad, which was used to create blue dyes prior to being replaced by indigo following the discovery of sea routes to India. Erfurt also played host to two East-West summits. At the 1808 Congress of Erfurt, Napoleon attempted to form a powerful alliance between France and Russia at the expense of England, Austria, and Prussia. The second, in 1970, featured East German Prime Minister Willi Stoph and West German Chancellor Willy Brandt, who met during early attempts to ease Cold War tension.

Perhaps, most emblematically, Erfurt provided the educational and early monastic home to Martin Luther, initiator of the Reformation and ranked third by *Life* on its list of most influential people of the past millennium, right behind fellow countryman and printing press inventor Johannes Gutenberg and Atlantic-crossing Christopher Columbus. While Luther traveled a good deal in Germany and those places he visited have a bit of the "George Washington slept here" boastfulness and frequency, Luther lived in Erfurt for over a decade. He attended the Universität Erfurt, which was founded in 1392, a hundred years before Columbus laid eyes on the West Indies, and hailed as one of the leading liberal arts institutions in all of Europe during the fifteenth and sixteenth centuries. Luther once proclaimed, "If you want a good education, go to Erfurt." Apparently, not enough heeded his advice. The university slowly lost students and prestige until its eventual closing in 1816. As part of the city's restoration after forty years of communist neglect, the university was reestablished in 1994, reappropriating what had been a teacher training school during GDR times.

Interestingly, one can still visit an Erfurt very similar to the one known to Luther. Erfurt has been described as the most well-preserved medieval city in Germany, having been almost completely spared the bombings of World War II that so decimated other German cities. Many of the medieval features survived communist times not because of a preservationist movement but because there simply was not enough money to renovate or repair dwellings.

We would come to find that this capital of the Thuringian

state also has a defiant streak despite its having been one of the three cities from which the Stasi ran its operations. Across from the train station sits the Erfurter Hof, a hotel that predated the GDR and obviously had been, at one time, quite stately but which stood empty when we arrived. The hotel played host to those early negotiations at East-West reconciliation between Prime Minister Stoph and Chancellor Brandt. According to Wilfried, as the two emerged to announce the new, tension-relieving *Ostpolitik*, a chant arose from the large gathering of East Germans. The crowd of comrades shouted, "Willi! Willi! Willi!" Or perhaps it was "Willy! Willy! Willy!" And so the ever-present Stasi, standing nearby, could only watch silently as these East Germans in all likelihood openly defied their government while seeming to support it.

In Erfurt's Domplatz, a pair of tri-spired churches that rise high into the sky from atop a hill also shows the citizens' audaciousness. Because the Archbishop of Mainz, who built the Mariendom, or St. Mary's Cathedral, visited here infrequently, the people of Erfurt built their own church, St. Severus, right next to it. While its plain design is not as eye-catching as the ornate gothic style of Mariendom, St. Severus's spires reach almost as high, claiming near equality with the bishop's cathedral. Indeed, for four centuries St. Severus rose higher than Mariendom, since the latter's towers burned down in 1454 and were not rebuilt until 1854.

Across from the cathedral square, or Domplatz, one can find the current police headquarters. Prior to the Wall collapsing, the building housed the Stasi headquarters for all of southwestern East Germany. Again, reflective of their temerity, Erfurt citizens were the first in the East to storm a Stasi headquarters after the Wall fell, assuring the preservation of the documents and other evidence within.

On the ride from the train station to our new home, our female taxi driver avoided all these landmarks in the pedestrian-only zone and instead took us out to the city's northern edge via a spur. Having a female taxi driver and a Mercedes for a cab provided some of the first incongruities we would encounter in the east. Upon turning a corner to enter our neighborhood, we were confronted by another. We drove past what appeared to be an American-style mall complete with atrium-style facade, a grand entrance, and a fountain out front.

From the interior of the cream-colored Mercedes, we first glimpsed our neighborhood of gray and tan *Plattenbau* apartment buildings. In this area that could hold a good-sized city's worth of inhabitants, I counted three designs: tall, seventeen-story cubes set on angles to the streets; eleven-story structures two to three blocks long with hundreds of balconies facing the road; and squat, four-story buildings that formed U's around a commons area. In the 1970s, when these Soviet-style apartments were constructed—prefabricated concrete plates stacked one upon another (hence *Plattenbau*, literally "plate" or "panel" building)—they were wildly popular, offering central heat and a bathroom in each apartment. Prior to this, the norm was coal brought up from the basement and a shared toilet down the hall.

A few turns later, the driver pulled into a cul-de-sac and stopped before one of the four-story buildings. As she unloaded our luggage from the trunk, we all looked at our new home. Drab yellow paint peeled from the concrete windbreak surrounding the door. While bushes and flowers decorated the fronts of some buildings, ours faced an open area of concrete. Weeds pushed up from between cracks. Two more concrete blocks served as benches. Any non-modernist aesthetic sense was frowned upon in the communist state. Doc-

trine argued that a more decorative beauty would awaken a bourgeoisie vanity, encouraging people to compete with one another for the most beautiful items. Clearly, no one had attempted to change that situation here since the Wall's fall.

The driver accepted the fare and tip, got back in her car, and began to pull away. I wanted to run after the taxi and hail her. But what would I say? Where could she take us? Instead, I turned back to Roberta and smiled. She tried to smile back. On our trip from Regensburg to Weimar, the group had also visited Erfurt for a day. We could have visited our neighborhood but chose not to. Just as we chose not to find out Callan's sex before she was born, Roberta and I decided to wait until we were moving in to see our home for the first time. I was grateful we had; we might have been looking forward to our arrival much less had we already seen this area.

We hauled our bags over to the door and entered using the key we had been provided. Impossibly, the entryway with its speckled granite floor was even more drab than the outside. It was unclear whether the color of the walls, papered an off-white-verging-on-brown, was intentional or the result of aging. Small metal lockers served as mailboxes, the corner of one folded back by someone trying to pry out the contents. Against the back wall, hidden fluorescent lights provided indirect illumination of the area. The far end of the stairwell was equally grimy. A sense of dread, as heavy as the drabness of the landing, further descended on me, making the bags even more difficult to carry up the stairs. The trip from bright Berlin to colorless Dessau was being repeated: from colorful Erfurt to our drab apartment building. I wanted to open one of our suitcases and crawl into it, just as that woman escaping the GDR had done long ago. Instead, I slipped the key into the lock of the hollow-core door and listened as the rattling echoed through the hallway.

Though we had spent six weeks taking our language course in the enchanting medieval town of Regensburg in the west, we were ready to leave because we had spent that time living in two small dorm rooms sandwiched around a miniscule eat-in kitchen and bath. That kitchen was less than three feet wide and not much longer. Each apartment was normally shared by two students; we doubled the capacity. The bedrooms were so small I was actually given a room of my own far down the hall, where I was supposed to spend my nights in a single bed in an otherwise empty room. Roberta and I did not intend to spend six weeks sleeping alone, so we dragged my bed down to her room and pushed the two together. Once the beds were wedged into the small room, we could not open the door of the white pressboard armoire. Nor was it possible to get through the hallway door. We could exit only by walking through the small kitchen to the kids' room and using their door. We had Callan sleep on a mattress on their floor so we could shove it under the other bed during the day, creating the only open floor space in the whole suite.

Thus, we had been looking forward to leaving for our *Plattenbau* in the east. We knew it would not come close to the size of our modest, twelve-hundred-square-foot home in New Jersey. Yet, after the dorm rooms we were sure we would feel like we were roaming free. Now, I turned the key with trepidation as I feared the apartment would be as dreary and uninviting as the entry and stairs. Being a family *im Aufbruch* scared me now. We crossed the threshold into our new life: from American to German, from west to east, from past to present, and from present to future.

My immediate reaction was one of relief. Size-wise, the apartment fit our needs: bedrooms for each of the kids with beds that folded up to create more floor space during the day; a room for Roberta and me with its king-size bed, which we could walk around, if just barely; an entrance hallway, kitchen, and large dining/living area; even a small balcony at one end of the living area. Here we stored our beer in winter, Roberta grew a container garden in spring, and we often perched ourselves to watch life pass by a floor below us, our refuge from the apartment without having to venture too far into the outside world.

Storage space abounded with wardrobes and shelves everywhere we looked. Plus, the place was fully furnished, as the landlords planned to be in the United States for only a year. Because they had two kids, all sorts of toys remained behind. And of course there was the computer, the VCRs, and the television with the large pizza-box sized screen, which even offered CNN, NBC, and MTV in English.

But our enthusiasm for the relative size of the apartment was dampened by its contents. Gray-flecked carpeting that seemed stained with the dirt of decades crawled several inches up the walls where, instead of molding defining its edge, the rug ended in a jagged cut. Stucco wallpaper, which overlapped the carpeting, adhered to the concrete walls. Several of the overhead lights did not rest against the ceiling but instead were suspended by spliced wires. Likewise, the door buzzer hung against the wall, dangling from its wires. Dark, fiberboard cabinets covered in fake-wood contact paper filled the windowless kitchen. Because neither of the two kitchen outlets was near where one would want to plug things in, the microwave cord ran behind the sink. Since most rooms contained only one outlet, extension cords were part of the décor.

The more we looked, the worse our second impression became. When we left New Jersey, we had spent weeks preparing our house for the couple subletting it. We cleaned the house thoroughly. We relocated everything that could be moved to the basement or the garage, removing the touches that made the home ours but would not be wanted by the renters. We bought three hundred dollars' worth of supplies: light bulbs, vacuum bags, borough-regulated orange trash bags. We even purchased a dryer, an appliance we had never owned but thought would be expected by a renter.

Apparently, our landlords did not feel they had the same responsibility toward their subletters. She, an East German, and he, an expatriated American, had left only the day before. In a bit of a misunderstanding on my part, we had arrived a day early, so the woman's mother did not have much of a chance to do her planned cleaning. That might have explained the laundry hamper that held several pieces of dirty clothes, including a pair of men's stretched and fading jockey shorts. And it might have explained why food, including spoiling leftovers, remained on the refrigerator shelves. But the bed in Roberta's and my room turned out to have only box springs; there was no mattress. And each of the many cabinets and drawers scattered throughout the living area and bedrooms was filled with the detritus of the family who had just left: papers, photos, clothes, extension cords, old letters. They had seemingly disappeared, as if hauled away by the Stasi, and we were being asked to assume their lives.

Between the time we dropped our few bags on the floor and the time we began to call this place home, we noticed more about the apartment. Many things were crooked. While some of these are understandable—mirrors, paintings, and knick-knacks hanging on the walls—we also found installed items that were askew. One of the kitchen drawers constantly fell into the one below it, and many of the cabinet doors did not shut correctly. To have a cabinet stay closed, the one next to it would have to be opened then the two pushed shut simultaneously. Even then, since so much was not plumb, one might walk in to find the doors ajar, as if someone recently in the kitchen had left in hurry. The radiators, which attached to the wall and had been installed when the building was constructed, were also off plumb.

The bathroom was the most fascinating part of the apartment. The sink and mirrored cabinet above it were, as expected, hung crookedly. There was no shower curtain and no rod on which to hang one. The silver wallpaper was peeling off, the mold below causing it to pull away. Behind a large sheet of wallpapered metal hid the rusting underside of the ceramic-lined tub. Yet the bathroom was a model of efficiency. Not even six feet by six feet, it contained, in addition to the full-sized tub, a toilet, sink, floor-to-ceiling cupboard, and clothes washer. And there was still room to stand. Accommodating all this required the overlapping of some functions. To fill the bathtub, one had to rotate the sink's spigot over the tub. The washer drained its dirty water directly into the tub as well, which meant that one could not bathe and wash clothes at the same time. The bathroom represented the epitome of cramped efficiency and ugliness. Like the East German state, it provided everything, if inconveniently, while leaving no room to turn.

Plattenbau have become popular in Berlin, where the Fernsehturm stands like a giant baton ready to conduct its dwindling orchestra. Not only is there a *Plattenbau* museum and a hostel called the Ostel (*Ost* plus *hostel*), but some people find them trendy to live in. They decorate with retro furniture from the socialist era, recreating the look and feel of an East German apartment from generations past. Those West Berliners who find it chic to live in the former East refer to themselves as "refugees." I am convinced that only those who remember the GDR through the innocent eyes of childhood or never lived there at all find this lifestyle so quaint.

And yet we had nothing to complain about. Like the Berlin *Plattenbau* dwellers, we chose this dwelling. We had wanted to see how eastern Germans lived. We decided on this more realistic experience over the one offered by the university guesthouse, a newly renovated medieval building located downtown but situated at the edge of our price range. Had we really wanted to stay there, we could have cut other corners. But price wasn't what caused us to make this decision. We wanted to live like, not simply among, the former East Germans. We wanted to send our kids to local German schools, not the international school a town away. We wanted to shop where the citizens of Erfurt shopped. *Plattenbau* living offered a base camp from which to explore the experience we sought.

We also decided to do very few typical tourist activities. We did not take any brewery tours or visit the fairytale castle Neuschwanstein. We did not even leave the former East Germany until late in our stay because we felt it would be possible to live in a place for a year and still be nothing more than a tourist. We did not want that. Instead, we spent our time discovering as much as we could about Erfurt and visiting small towns in the east. We are homebodies at heart, and we tried to be homebodies in Erfurt, to see what it would be like to live in post-reunification eastern Germany.

Obviously, my family could not exactly live the East German experience, since those times were past, but we probably came as close as Americans could nearly a dozen years after reunification. We saw a culture not only *as it is* but influenced greatly by *as it was*. While all cultures carry their own historical baggage, when society's basic foundations have been so drastically altered, as in eastern Germany, the relics from that previous time stand out more. We were like astronomers who, with their telescopes capturing light that began traveling billions of years before, witness events that occurred long ago. Looking at east Germany through our telescope of the present, we knew that distant star had ceased to exist. Yet, by spending an extended period of time in the east, we caught a glimpse of what went on in those distant galaxies of the GDR.

Of course, all societies—and individuals—do not look through the same telescopes. Much more so than the narrative of the U.S. government, which has been stable for well over two centuries now, in Germany, especially in eastern Germany, people had lived under four regimes: the Weimar Republic, the Third Reich, communism, and democracy. Concepts of past and memory are effervescent, ephemeral, conflicted, contentious even, as seen in the debates that took place over who should have access to Stasi files, an embarrassing remnant of the GDR. Few systems go as far as the communists of East Germany, who built the Wall, in part, to keep their people from experiencing worldviews other than the one they propagated, yet each society offers its own way of seeing the world.

Six months later, we realized how much we had internalized the *Ossie* perspective when we took the train to visit Roberta's retired engineer uncle and aunt in Hamburg. They lived just outside the city in a beautiful home that rivaled in size, and dwarfed in quality, most American houses. We had become so used to the eastern lifestyle and its almost monochromatic tones that we were overwhelmed by Hamburg's vibrancy. In the city, the people moved quickly and with purpose. They laughed and chattered happily. We oohed and ahhed at the uncountable colors and creations of capitalism. We even bought ourselves a new camera to take photos of this more highly defined west. Our fading white, eastern T-shirt had been replaced by tie-dye. We were both amazed and appalled by the choices, the possibilities, our own desires. In short, I believe we behaved as East Germans must have when, with the opportunity to finally visit the West, they found it nothing less than breathtaking.

4. Concrete Details
Your Guide's Tour of Erfurt

Come with me. I want to show you some things. It's a short tour. We won't be gone long.

It starts here outside the *Plattenbau* I'm living in. Notice the concrete. It's all concrete: walls, floors, ceilings. Pre-formed apartments stacked one on top of another during former times.

Look around. This once was farm fields on the edge of town. Now *Plattenbau* everywhere. Three hundred altogether in Erfurt—enough housing for over half of the town's 235,000 inhabitants when the Wall came down. They were built so that everyone had a place to live out the busy but uneventful lives the state had planned for them.

Following the collapse of the Wall and an initial influx of West Germans—brought in to run businesses, teach at the university, and administer everything else—housing in Erfurt was so tight that costs were the third highest in Germany, trailing only Munich and Hamburg. Since then, almost 40,000 people have left, gone west across the former border in search of jobs and new lives. By 2020, another 30,000 are expected to leave. The population then will be 168,000. To combat this—and stay above the 200,000 threshold that means additional government monies—Erfurt keeps annexing nearby towns and villages, a physical bloating of the city. New construction and the renovation of old-city apartments now make *Plattenbau* the least desirable housing. With no people to fill them, dozens of the *Plattenbau* in Erfurt are slated for demolition over the next few years. More than half a century after World War II, the destruction begins anew.

Look there and there. And there. No drapes. So many empty apartments. Mostly it is the young who move, leaving the older generation behind. And alone. Nearly 40 percent of the housing in Erfurt contains only one person. Of those who remain, many spend their time looking out the windows. See that man up there with the gray hair, elbows on the sill? Since the windows are hinged like doors and there are no screens, he can just lean out. Even in winter, he has the window open. I see him every day—watching, pondering, trying to make sense from up high. Do you think he ever gets the urge to jump? Others have.

We're standing on the corner of Moskauerstrasse and Sofioterstrasse. All the streets in this area are named for capitals of once-communist or Soviet-leaning countries. In addition to Moscow and Sofia, streets are named after Havana and Hanoi, Bucharest and Budapest, Prague and Warsaw, even Vilnius and Ulan Bator, the capitals of Lithuania and Mongolia—and of course Berlin. This refers to what we know as East Berlin, but the GDR never called it by that name. Doing so would require conceding that there was also a West Berlin, somehow delegitimizing the country. The Strasse der Nationen, the Street of Nations, that runs through the midst of these streets, further signifies the eminence the GDR gave these countries.

Here comes the *Strassenbahn*. Quick. Make a run for it. That bell means the doors are going to close. Emphatic,

aren't they? Notice how the Germans trust one another. No one to take your money. It is expected that you will buy a ticket. There are occasional spot checks. I have been asked only once in my time here. I have never seen anyone who didn't have the required ticket when it was requested.

This is our stop. Universität. Come, I want to show you where I spend my days.

Through these gates. Odd that the university is fenced in, isn't it? This was all erected when the college's only mission was to train teachers, who would in turn train young people to become good GDR citizens. Wave to the security guard in the booth when he looks up from the surveillance camera. It's his job to know everyone.

Here's my building. More concrete. Let's take the stairs. I always take the stairs. My office is on the sixth floor. Since the first floor is not numbered here in Germany, that would be the seventh in the U.S. We Germans and Americans regard our stories differently.

Go ahead; catch your breath. My office is down the hall, last door on the left. Come inside. Quite a view out the window, no? I want you to see something. Out there. On the hill,

where it begins to slope downward. Use these binoculars. That's why I keep them here. Can you see it better now?

That's the Buchenwald Memorial, 165 feet of concrete. About seventeen stories high, same as some of the *Plattenbau*. On clear days, the monument is visible from everywhere in the surrounding area. Here, we're about ten miles away. The monument stands a short distance from the entrance to Buchenwald Concentration Camp, which is hidden by the trees. At its base are eighteen smaller stone pillars, each representing the nations from which camp prisoners came. The walk in front of the pillars is also called Strasse der Nationen. It traverses depressions in the ground that were once filled with the cremated remains of prisoners.

Some 238,000 people passed through the gates of Buchenwald—as prisoners. Equivalent to Erfurt's population at its height. A fifth did not come out alive. Official camp estimates place the total death toll at 65,000—approximately the number of people who will have vacated Erfurt by 2020.

You can see stone and concrete at Buchenwald, too. The

main access to the camp is called the Road of Blood to com-
memorate the many prisoners, mostly Jews, who died while
being forced, during its construction, to transport stones
from a nearby quarry. Those who bore rocks the SS judged
too small were immediately killed.

Within the camp, rows of concrete foundations where
wooden barracks once stood are now filled with rocks taken
from the quarry. Also, a wide strip of stones bordering the
fence delimits the "neutral zone," an area where prisoners
were not allowed to tread. Those who did were shot.

My colleague Andreas—he's German—wanted to visit Buchenwald Camp and the memorial shortly after he
moved to town. He's one of the few coming into Erfurt rather than leaving. Being unfamiliar with the area, he stopped
at a village in the valley below the monument and asked several people for directions. Not one could tell him what route
to take to reach the monument. Perhaps this corroborates

Austrian writer Robert Musil's claim that "there is nothing in this world as invisible as a monument."

We should be going. If we hurry, we can catch the 3:15 *Strassenbahn* into town. Along the way, we'll pass the local jail, a dark red brick building looming behind a fifteen-foot stone wall that once served as Stasi headquarters. We can also walk to J. A. Topf and Sons, the factory where they made the crematoria used in Buchenwald and Auschwitz. It remained in business, under various guises, until 1994. Now it is no more than an empty compound of brick and concrete structures standing in a neighborhood of nice apartments. Neither of these sites can be found on tourist maps.

Just out this door, down the stairs, then back out through the gates. Wave to the guard again. He's doing his job.

Follow me.

5. ALFs, Autos, and Encounters with the *Polizei*

One early Friday morning in December, a couple months into our Erfurt stay, I left our apartment for the university. I walked down the flight of steps and let the entry door shut behind me. Since Erfurt is situated north of the entire continental United States, I entered eight o'clock predawn darkness. The morning was cold and foggy. I passed under the arch that separated our building from the next and headed for the streetcar stop a block away. In this dark dampness, the blues, yellows, and blacks of the cars glistened.

I was halfway across Sofioterstrasse when it struck me. Not a car, but a thought. And the thought was that for almost two weeks I had walked past our red 1992 Ford Escort on my way to and from work. But standing in the middle of the street, replaying through my mind's eye, I was sure that the car I had just walked past was blue. As if a character in a B-grade horror movie, I slowly turned around. A blue Fiesta sat in the spot where we had left our red Escort.

I say "ours" but really the car belonged to the family we sublet the apartment from. For a nominal fee added to the rent, we were allowed to use their aged Ford. We drove it infrequently, using it only for weekend trips to other towns. But it fit our lifestyle. We could get up at a reasonable hour

on a Saturday or Sunday and visit a neighboring village or three before driving home. By doing so, we avoided the twenty-five-minute streetcar ride to the train station and being tied to the train's thin weekend schedule. We could change plans during the middle of the journey. We could come and go as we pleased. "Our" car was a luxury we appreciated having.

But we hadn't gone anywhere for a couple weeks, and so the Escort should have been where we left it. I looked up and down the road with trepidation. When these apartment houses were built during East German times, fewer people owned cars, so parking was not a problem. Now, with more cars, people fight for spots on the street as if this were a large city. Once a spot is abandoned, it is soon taken. I recalled having parked the car in front of two large recycling dumpsters. The blue car was now in front of them. Wait, I spied a red car behind the dumpsters. Maybe they had been emptied and put back in a different spot. But the red car was not an Escort. It was not our car. I looked up the road. A red Escort!

Relieved, I walked up to it. Four doors like ours, old like ours, same wheels. Wrong license plate number. I set off again. Had we driven the car somewhere that I had forgotten about and parked it elsewhere? No, our last trip was two weekends ago. I was sure we hadn't taken it anywhere since then.

I went back to the apartment and met Roberta at the door.

"Did you forget something?" she asked.

"No, we have a bigger problem," I replied. "The car is gone."

She needed to see for herself. She hurried out to the balcony and looked down to where the car had been.

"How could someone take it from there? It was right in front of the apartment!"

We went over it again. Had we driven the car recently? Were we sure that was where we parked it? Were we not permitted to park it there? Had it been towed because it was too close to the dumpsters? Can one leave a car unmoved only for a certain amount of time before it gets towed? Or had it really been stolen? Whatever the answers to these questions, we knew the car was gone, and we needed to find out where it was.

When one accepts the opportunity to live in a foreign country, there are many uninvited situations one hopes to avoid. These would be problematic at home, but even more so when one isn't comfortable with the language and unsure of the cultural norms. Having one's car stolen, to me, fell into one of these avoid-at-all-costs incidents. So my immediate reaction was to call the International Office at the university, whose staff had been so helpful since we arrived. I reached Ingrid. Despite the Germanic name, Ingrid, with dark hair and complexion, was born and raised in Columbia. She had studied journalism in the United States, where she met her husband, Frank Schumacher, a German getting his doctorate in North American history. They had come to Erfurt when Frank accepted an assistant professor position at the university.

After listening to my story, Ingrid assured me that I must have parked the car elsewhere and that I just needed to look around for it. I knew she was wrong, but I also knew that no one would believe me until I had done a thorough search. After all, why would anyone steal an eight-year-old dented Escort with ninety thousand kilometers on it? Even by the scaled-down expectations of east Germans, the car wasn't appealing. Other than a couple of the East German–made Trabants still puttering around the neighborhood, I had seen few cars less worthy of thievery. I realized that my claim of the Escort heist must have sounded absurd, so I agreed to search the neighborhood. Roberta and I spread out and scoured different streets. When we met up ten minutes later, each of us had come across a red Escort, neither of them ours.

Following a series of phone calls between Ingrid, Frank, and me, Ingrid reached the police and was informed that the car had not been towed. They too suggested we might have simply forgotten where we had parked it. Frank relayed the story of a friend who had parked his car, forgotten where he left it, and then reported it stolen. I had also been told about a man who had driven his car downtown when he usually took the streetcar. After a night of drinking, he took the tram home. The next morning he discovered his car "missing" and called the police to report it stolen. Only when the police found it four weeks later in town, locks untouched and in good shape, did the man recall having parked it there prior to his inebriation. Of course, he never revealed this to the authorities, instead thanking them for "recovering" his vehicle. The Erfurt police, perhaps familiar with such scenarios, suggested a thorough search. We assured them it had already been conducted, so they told us to pay them a visit.

Since reaching the police station in our area of town required taking a streetcar into the city center and another back out again, Ingrid and Herr Nuremberg, a colleague of hers in the International Office who owned a car, offered to accompany me. Herr Nuremberg exemplified the eastern German economic situation. Having lost his job under the new system, he applied for a work program in which businesses or government entities are provided a worker at low cost for six or twelve months. The person supplies temporary help while gaining practical experience in a situation that might lead to a job either there or elsewhere.

Herr Nuremberg's job at the university was to create a Web page for the International program. The problem was that Herr Nuremberg didn't know much about html or computers for that matter. The Web page project progressed slowly throughout the months I was there, and when the time came to decide whether to retain Herr Nuremberg for six more months, he was let go, even at such a low wage. The situation represented old East Germany clashing with new east Germany, a worker unable to recreate himself in an economy that demanded it of him.

But at the time, Herr Nuremberg—I never knew his first name; he was only referred to by his last name, which remains a common custom among coworkers in Germany—was still working for the university, so it was in an Escort much like our missing one that I was driven to the police station. This turned out to be a good thing because I would never have found it by myself. Housed in an area that appeared to be part of an office complex, the station was unmarked and unidentifiable until one drove into the parking lot behind the building and out of the fog appeared several green and white Opels with blue lights on top and *Polizei* stenciled across the doors, hood, and trunk.

From the parking lot, we entered through a back door, where we found a building directory inconspicuously announcing the second-floor police station. We took the stairs and followed the signs down a hallway. We passed two officers headed out, already smoking their morning cigarettes.

Once inside the station, we stood before a Formica counter that ran the width of the room. The woman ahead of us was quite upset. She had called about a loud party in her neighborhood a few evenings ago, but the police had never shown up. She wanted to file a complaint against the police. The officer listened and nodded, his arms spread, hands on the edge of the counter. When the woman finally gave him the chance to speak, he explained that she was welcome to fill out the form—if he could find one—but that it probably would never receive a response. They were already understaffed and so they often couldn't respond to a minor event such as the one she called in, and this understaffing also meant that her complaint would probably receive similar treatment. Throughout the explanation and follow-up exchange, the woman became more and more agitated. The officer remained calm. Finally, she threw up her arms and walked out.

Now it was our turn. Ingrid relayed our story. We were told to take a seat in the waiting room across the hall. Filled with cheap tables and chairs, Coke and candy machines, and posters, the room resembled a small employees' cafeteria more than a waiting area. The carpeting was gray-white, cheap and dirty.

After an indeterminate amount of time in which we exhausted conversation, magazines, and curiosity in those sharing the room, I was staring at the grayness of the outside and the parking lot when we were summoned forth by a mustached officer in green pants and mustard yellow shirt with epaulets. As the officer held open the door to the inner rooms of the station, I walked back eight years into my only other encounter with the German police.

During my tour of the former East with Jim Soderholm in 1992, our travels took us into the center of Leipzig. Arriving late in the evening, we did not even bother to search for the more quaint but harder-to-find *pensions* and instead booked ourselves into the first hotel we saw. Tired, we grabbed our bags, went upstairs, and fell into our beds.

In the morning, we returned downstairs for breakfast. The dining room, which had been a dark, music-filled discotheque when we had passed by the night before, was now soaked in early sunlight that poured through the floor-to-ceiling windows running the length of two sides. We found a table next to the window and sat in the warmth of the sun. Cloth-covered tables, hot coffee, and the traditional array of meats, cheeses and rolls awaited us. That this looked exactly like so many other German breakfast rooms reinforced my belief that whatever differences existed between East and West before the Wall came down had dissolved in the reunified Germany.

Tearing a bite from a roll, I glanced out the window and noticed a man looking at our rented VW Golf parked across the street from where we sat. Okay, I thought to myself, maybe everything is not the same if a West German Volkswagen was still enough of an oddity to cause so much interest. The man walked on and I continued eating.

A few minutes later, another man walking past the car stopped and peered inside. This time I looked more closely at the scene. Even through the driver's side, I could see jagged glass edges framing the passenger-side window.

"Scheisse!" I said, employing my limited German vocabulary. "Shit!" I repeated for Jim, my non-German-speaking companion.

I jumped up from the table, ran out the front door, and made my way across the street ahead of Jim. We had left cassette tapes, a couple of jackets, even some change in the car. Everything remained, albeit covered in a spray of glass. The interior seemed untouched. I looked around the outside of the car. Nothing but more glass.

I couldn't understand why someone would just break the window of a car. Had the thief been interrupted before anything could be removed? Was someone, perhaps leaving the discotheque and, emboldened by alcohol, showing off to friends? I wouldn't find out the most probable scenario until I returned to Giessen and spoke with a German friend of mine.

"It's the license plate," Barbara said upon my telling her the story. When I didn't register any recognition, she reminded me that the letters that begin German license plates identify where the car is registered: M for Munich, HH for Hamburg, B for Berlin. I knew this, so I must have looked like a young innocent as she went on to ask, "And what did your license plate begin with?"

"GI," I said, recalling paperwork on the car.

"And . . . ?" she asked.

"And GI stands for Giessen," I said, still not getting it.

"And where is Giessen?"

"Germany," I replied confidently.

"Good," she said slowly enough to let me know that was not the correct answer.

"Okay, West Germany."

Barbara slapped the table. "Now, you've got it. Every time my boyfriend goes over there for his business, he comes home with broken windows, too. There are still a lot of angry people over there. And the kids can do nothing but take it out on the cars from the west. You rented the car in the west, so it had western plates."

And, I figured out on my own, this is why nothing was taken from the car. The vandals could have stolen everything, but that would have then made burglary the motive for breaking the window. By taking nothing, we were to understand this as a statement, not as a crime of need. It probably would not have mattered to the criminals that we were Americans rather than Germans. The crime was committed against westerners, no matter their country of origin. Those responsible were simply angry about the peaceful overthrow that turned East Germany into east Germany.

After verifying that nothing was stolen, Jim and I went back inside the hotel and called the rental company. We were told that if we wanted to get a new vehicle for the remainder of the trip and not be responsible for the damages to this one, we would have to file a police report. Another inconvenience, we thought, but we couldn't spend the whole trip with one window open. The hotel clerk informed us that both a police substation and a local branch of the rental car agency were within a few blocks. We could file the report, trade cars, and be on our way.

We quickly found the police station. The building itself was innocuous-looking enough. In the middle of a row of similar attached structures that included apartments and a few shops, the stone façade was simple and unadorned. No sign stated the building's function. We might have missed the station if not for the green and white police van parked directly in front. The Germans, it seems, are good at concealing their police stations.

Inside, the lobby appeared to have received recent but poor remodeling. A white drywall booth had been roughed

out around the small reception desk. Seams were visible under a light coat of white paint, and the window the officer opened to speak with us grabbed as he slid it. In my weak German, I began to tell our story to the policeman. He nodded a couple of times, cut me off and, pointing to a waiting room to the side, told us to take a seat.

An elderly couple, pale and lifeless, already cowered on hardback chairs. Both appeared to have entered a catatonic state as a means to cope with the waiting. As we sat down across from them, the two slowly rotated their heads to stare at us. We waited. The couple became bored with staring and turned their attention to the walls. These were bare and already scuffed from shoe marks along the bottom. The tile floors were unswept and unpolished. We waited some more. Jim and I spoke little, our non-German conversation an awkwardness that filled the room.

The desk officer didn't seem to have much to do except disappear periodically for several minutes at a time. Whenever he returned, he fell heavily into his chair and sipped on a cola. A young couple of Middle Eastern descent entered and spoke with him. He directed the couple to wait with us. They huddled together in their own corner of the room. Agitated about whatever had happened to them and talking rapidly in their native tongue, the two appeared more comfortable than Jim and I at playing the role of foreigner.

Finally, the young man turned to the rest of the group. "Wie lange warten Sie?" he asked. How long have you been waiting?

I looked at my watch. For us, it had been only forty-five minutes, not long compared to the older couple, who said they had been there almost two hours.

While we were comparing times, the door leading to the back of the station banged open and out stepped an officer. As if called to attention, those of us in the waiting room sat upright. The man wore the mustard yellow shirt and green pants I'd seen so often on police officers in Giessen. More than being a coincidence, I was sure the police on this side of the Wall had been made to adopt the uniform of the West. The man at the door wasn't young. Had he been a police officer during East German times, or had he come into the force with the change of uniform? Was a police officer seen as simply an enforcer of a system's laws, no matter what the system, or were East German police officers too tied to the legacy of the communist regime and therefore let go? Was he an import from the west? Had he been in the Stasi?

The officer called out the elderly couple's last name, and they disappeared behind the door. A little while later, the young couple gave up and walked out. I looked at my watch. We had been in the room well over an hour. Jim and I discussed leaving, but we decided that we had put in our time for this long and didn't think it would be worth having to pay for the damage, so we waited. But we talked little, still conscious of not speaking German in this bare room.

Finally, the door opened and we were summoned forward. The officer standing at the door, small and thin, wore the ubiquitous policeman's uniform of mustache on the upper lip and holstered pistol at his side. After the door clanked shut behind us, the man directed us to follow him. We were close to getting our replacement car. The long hallway had not undergone remodeling, and my judgment of the repairs out front changed. It looked much better than this dimly lit hall where the yellowed walls appeared to have accumulated years of smoke and dust. Our footsteps echoed off the floor. Jim and I exchanged a look.

We walked past many closed doors but stopped to enter none of them. One door stood open, and I caught a glimpse of the older couple huddled in two chairs before a small desk, an officer sitting behind. It was difficult to tell whether the couple was seeking help or being interrogated.

At the end of the hall, the man turned left and began to walk down another hallway. At the end of this one, he turned right and kept passing rooms. A door stood at the end of this hall and, upon reaching it, the man opened it and escorted us through. We had entered another hallway. We walked some more, turned another left, then turned a quick right that placed us at our destination.

We stood in what appeared to be a classroom. Rows of veneer-topped tables were screwed to the floor, with hardback wooden chairs pushed underneath. We were directed to sit at the end of the first row, facing a brown chalkboard. The man pulled another chair around to face us. Was this how it was during GDR times? Is this where the police, or the Stasi even, were trained in methods of keeping the populace under control? What lay hidden beneath the erasures on the chalkboard?

The policeman asked us to explain our situation. I did

so in my halting, error-filled German. Jim's knowledge of German was limited to a very few words, so he sat silently but pretended to listen intently. A few sentences into my recounting, the door opened and another man stepped in. He was larger than the first officer, doughier and more waxen.

"Didn't you bring it?" the first asked his colleague in German.

"No," the new man responded.

"Can you get it?"

The door closed again and the man asked me to continue with the story. But soon, the second officer pushed open the door with his back. He waddled in, hefting a typewriter—old, black, nonelectric. The keyboard was terraced high, each key ringed in metal. It appeared this machine could have seen use before the initials GDR were ever typed together to represent a communist country.

The man heaved the typewriter onto the desk, swore to himself and disappeared again. He soon returned with paper—white and carbon. He dropped himself into the chair facing us, placed a sheet of carbon between two white sheets, tapped them against the desk, then rolled the paper sandwich into the machine.

He poised his fists above the keys, forefingers pointed, and began to type. The other three of us watched in silence until finally the typist told his companion he was ready.

We began with the details: names, addresses, citizenship, owner of the car, etc. But instead of just providing responses and having the man type them, we paused and waited between each as he seemingly tapped out more information than we had stated. Because those sheets of paper were blank, not only was he typing in the information we gave, but he also was creating the form itself.

Worse, since Jim was the one who had rented the car,

questions were directed at him. Once we got past the basics, Jim didn't understand the police officer. I would translate the questions, relaying the information to Jim. However, since I knew what Jim was going to say most of the time, being as familiar with the incident as he was, I eventually stopped translating and answered the questions myself with the help of the questioner, who was only too willing to fill in where I could not figure out how to explain what had happened. I was keen to accept anything he suggested be placed in the report if it would get us out of there more quickly. "Genau," I kept responding to his narrative additions. Exactly.

Five minutes into the recounting, the typist spat "Scheisse!" and tore the papers from the platen's grasp. He removed the carbon, then crumpled up the papers and threw them to the ground. Realizing this too was a mistake, he reached down and picked up the sheets, smoothing them beside his ancient typewriter. Whatever error he had made meant starting over, but he realized it was easier to copy that information than to ask us again.

As our typist gathered his new materials and two-fingered his way through the information again, I looked around the room. Dinginess pervaded: colorless walls made more so by burned-out bulbs overhead; dirty, barred windows overlooking a small, equally unattractive courtyard of cement; next to the chalkboard a gray bulletin board. On this were thumbtacked three items: a list of those who worked in the department with vacation dates next to their names and two ALF stickers. While I was curious as to how Müller and Rausch would spend their week off, it was the stickers that caught my attention.

Jim and I had crossed the Atlantic to reach Germany. We had traversed that border graphic over Uncle Walter's shoulder to discover what lay beneath that blank spot on the map of my—and I presume Jim's—youth. And we had traveled deep into the bowels of this police station that was possibly a Stasi office during GDR times—a building that represented the officiousness of the German Democratic state and which seemingly hadn't been cleaned since then—only to find fuzzy, caramel-colored ALF from American capitalist television society waving at us. The ALF series begins when a small creature piloting a spacecraft crashes into the Tanner family garage. He survives and becomes part of the household, with the Tanners calling him ALF, "alien life form." The show's storylines often focused on ALF's cultural differences and the problems he had fitting into a society he was quite literally not a part of. ALF premiered in 1986 and ended a few months before the fall of the Wall with the appropriately titled episode "Consider Me Gone."

I wondered if these stickers had been smuggled in during GDR times, a small insubordination that would probably only provoke laughs. Perhaps they served as reminders of the absurdity of the capitalist system. After all, who could fear an enemy that created goofy ALF? Maybe someone placed them there later, after the Wall's fall, a reminder to those stuck in the room that capitalism, like water, seeps through all cracks and into the most unexpected of places.

How the stickers got there is less important than their being there in the first place. They hinted that this young child-state was learning capitalism from its more experienced western sibling. But in such a situation one can't choose which behaviors will be accepted and which rejected. In having capitalism replace communism as the new ruling system, some of its less desirable traits accompanied it. One of capitalism's least attractive characteristics requires that along with the *haves*, there are always *have nots*. And, when the have nots see what the haves have, they are often resentful. They lash out. And for some have nots, the most obvious targets are those alien life forms whose presence signify the conquest of their former culture. Or, in Leipzig, the vehicle of those alien western life forms who dared to venture across that once-impenetrable border. And if we could breech this, I shouldn't have been surprised that ALF had also infiltrated the system, this symbol of capitalism over the shoulder of the police. We're in this together, he seemed to be saying with his goofy grin and upstretched arm.

At last, the typist pulled the final page from the typewriter. The report was finished. The other officer handed the papers to Jim, telling him to read them over and then sign.

Jim stared at the words for a moment before I jumped in. "Er versteht nicht," I offered. He doesn't understand. "But I'll translate."

I picked up the papers and began to read. Quickly, I went over the basic details and facts. Then there was a passage I didn't completely understand.

"I have no idea what this says, Jim, but I'll keep speaking in this tone of voice so they think I am reading to you." I pointed at the page.

"Okay, then this part here tells how we found out about the car and what it looked like when we found it. But I have no idea what this next sentence says. Or this one. Don't you think we've been here a long time. What do you think we should do once we get out of here." I made sure not to raise my voice at the end of the questions so that the police officers wouldn't recognize that I wasn't reading. My finger followed along on the page as I spoke.

"I also have no idea what this says. Or this." I looked at Jim who nodded appropriately. "Frankly, we just need to make our way through this, get it signed, and then we can take our copy and get out of here."

"Sounds good." Jim said. "Right."

After we "read" through the report, Jim signed, as did one of the policeman. We stood up, smiled, and shook hands all around, as if we had just completed a business transaction. I took one last look at ALF waving to us, this time goodbye, then we made our way back through the labyrinth, past the reception area, and out the door. Jim and I looked at each other and laughed as we tried to process what we had just experienced.

The Erfurt police station door clanged shut behind us. The policeman led us through another door that spanned the hallway. Though the hall was wider and the area better lit by florescent lights than the Leipzig police station, I couldn't help but think of that previous visit with Jim. This walk took us past open doors where uniformed officers sat at large white-topped desks speaking with those sitting across from them. Whether these people were reporting or being accused of crimes was again not clear at first glance. We finally turned and passed over a threshold that led into an office identical to the others.

This office was large, maybe twenty-five feet deep by fifteen feet wide. It contained the same ugly carpeting as the waiting room. Most of the room was empty. On the far side under the windows stood two large white tables, each with a computer on it. At least the technology had been upgraded since my Leipzig experience. Our man seated himself at one computer; a younger officer sat at the other, entering in handwritten data. Each hunted and pecked. The two men, I would learn when it rang, shared a phone that they pushed back and forth across the desks. There were two extra chairs. I was given the chair of honor next to the officer while Ingrid sat next to me and Herr Nuremberg leaned against the wall. The window blinds were open, but it had become so foggy out that the windows appeared to be their own wall. On the actual wall below the windows, a calendar. Nothing more.

This time I played the role of silent victim. Since Ingrid's German was much better than mine and Herr Nuremberg spoke no English, Ingrid served as my interpreter. The officer first asked what had happened, and Ingrid briefly explained my situation. The policeman turned to the computer, pulled up a file containing the proper form, and began tapping in the information he didn't need from us. He would then ask a question in German. Most of the early ones, I understood but allowed Ingrid to fulfill her role as translator, repeating them to me in English. When I began not to understand some of the harder questions, Ingrid began serving a real function. However, then came another easy question. I responded in German, but trilingual Ingrid became confused and translated my response into English, which she directed at the officer. Our chuckle for the morning.

After the form was complete, the man had to print out the report. While the daisy wheel whirred on the printer the two policemen shared, I turned in my chair and looked at the wall behind us. Except for some shoe smudges similar to those recently applied by Herr Nuremberg, the white wall was bare but for one small sheet thumbtacked to the drywall. I leaned closer to see what it said. Officer Schmidt's vacation days for the upcoming year were neatly typed onto the already graying paper.

The police found our car later that morning. The thief or thieves had taken it sometime in the night, driven about half a mile in the direction of the highway, lost control, and landed in a swampy area near the entrance ramp. Unable to free the vehicle, they simply left it, taking nothing. Yet the damage from jimmying the lock and door, along with the cracked windshield and bent undercarriage resulting from the accident, meant that the car, even though it didn't appear that way, was ultimately declared *Totalschaden*—totaled.

I saw the car that evening. The police had had it towed from under the bridge where it was found and taken it to a garage near the center of town. This time Frank accompanied me to the police station, from which we were driven to the garage in a police car.

At well over six feet in height, Frank folded himself into the back of the small Opel next to me. We drove along streets I did not recognize. The winter sun had set, and the darkness of the car was lit by the glow of the dash and the two-way radio.

A car rolled toward the stop sign on a cross street and continued on without ever coming to a halt. The two officers in front snickered and kept driving.

Frank asked the driver who he thought had stolen the car.

"Dumme Jungs," the man replied. Stupid boys. They have nothing to do, he explained. And Escorts are easy to break into. This wasn't a professional job. A 1992 Escort is not worth stealing if you want to part it out or send it to Poland or Russia, a common outcome of car theft in Germany. No, the officer hypothesized, these kids probably weren't even old enough to drive and were just taking the car out for a joyride.

Unprovoked, the man continued. "The problem," he complained, "is lack of leadership."

He and Frank continued to talk, but tired from the day's events, I turned to look outside at the passing cityscape. I conjured up the ALF stickers from eight years earlier. Because ALF was actually a large puppet controlled from below, he was often positioned behind a ledge or table. I imagined that, if it weren't so dark, to passersby I might resemble ALF—my head and shoulders rising above the doorframe—bewildered by this rare venture out of doors.

It was not until Frank and I were alone that he clarified the policeman's comment. A *Wessie* historian teaching at a university in the east, Frank understood the sociohistorical context that I had missed. In saying that the problem with youth today was that they lacked leadership, the police officer was contrasting "today" with before the Wall came down. Prior to then, the lives of youth were orchestrated by the Party. After-school activities were abundant. Community service projects were required, not voluntary, as they are in the U.S. The Jungpioniere, similar to our own scouting organizations with uniforms and rituals, served to indoctrinate youngsters into all things East German and communist. From early morning to evening, the Party found things for everyone to do. Such activities would build community among the citizens, keep them out of trouble, and allow them to watch over one another. If everyone is busy together, who has the time to think about overthrowing the state? For this officer, then, the *Wende* meant more trouble, more crimes, more work. The youth had nothing to keep them busy, no future prospects, and no respect for—let alone fear of—authority.

While this may not have made the officer happy, I found the progression from socialist to capitalist state reflected in these two incidents with the automobiles. When the window of the rental car was smashed in Leipzig shortly after the Wall fell, those who did so were lashing out. Their lives, their futures, their expectations had been turned up-

Augen auf

Keine Gewalt gegen ausländische Mitbürger dulden!

Helfen statt wegsehen.

CDU ERFURT

side down. The bland security of the East German state vanished abruptly, replaced with the fear-generating unknown and the imposition of capitalism by those who were the avowed enemy just a few months before. And, as often happens in such paradigm-shifting situations, unable to confront the system itself, the affected strike out at those who are close by, the ones they see as personifying the detested system.

This frustration did not subside readily. Living in Erfurt nearly a decade after that incident, we found that anti-foreigner sentiment was still prevalent enough that public-service billboards dotting the city proclaimed "Keep your eyes open. Don't tolerate violence against foreign citizens!"

But if I think the stolen Escort was about me, the foreigner, I am missing the point. The earlier Leipzig incident *was* about me. The VW's license plate announced us: foreign, uninvited, unwelcome, harbinger of change. The car provided a means to deliver the message: you are not wanted.

The Erfurt *dumme Jungs* were motivated differently. The act was all about the car and what it represented: freedom. They probably had not planned where they were going. There was no need since the freedom began as soon as they left the parking spot. Perhaps these youth started out heading nowhere—that joyride the policeman identified; freedom found not in the destination but in the driving itself—but they ended up attracted to the highway. The officer might have been mistaken. Maybe the youth were looking to use the highway to escape their already bleak lives.

It has often been said that if one wants to change the world, begin with the youth. They are still open to ideas their elders would reject. This is why we educate the young. It is why advertisers target young audiences. It is why the Jungpioniere looked a lot like the communist society of the adults. If I can get you when you're young, you are more likely to buy into my program and retain an allegiance to it. In the opening moments of capitalism in eastern Germany, the participants had grown up under a different set of rules. The Leipzig youth who smashed our window couldn't abide by the rules of the new game. Their moment of gullibility had passed. The youth who stole our car a decade later had grown up in the new system. They knew the rules, understood they weren't getting far if they played by them, and therefore stole the car. The acquisition, rather than the destruction, of the auto reflected their adopted capitalist inclinations.

In the Leipzig police station shortly after the Wall fell, ALF—Alien Life Form—represented so many things: western capitalist television, the invasion of foreign elements into East Germany, and the new foreigners being birthed and raised by this society—the ones our chauffeuring Erfurt policeman no longer recognized. When a society is in transition, ALFs are everywhere. Sometimes they look like *dumme Jungs*; sometimes they look like me.

6. Words Fail Me, Yet Again

I completed my day's teaching and left the university early one afternoon on my way to pick up Callan from kindergarten. When I reached the *Strassenbahn* stop, the electronic sign indicated that my streetcar would not arrive for another seven minutes. I leaned against the glass of the red metal shelter and looked past the campus buildings to the sun moving quickly toward the horizon in this northern winter sky.

As I waited for the streetcar on that uncommonly warm February day, I closed my eyes, hoping an idea for a short story would pop into my head. This, I knew, was fruitless. For me, writing requires something more akin to developing peripheral vision. Because the rods in our retinas are good at detecting motion but not color and because the rods are on the outside of our eyes, our peripheral vision is better in dim light. We then see most clearly those objects that are slightly off center. When we turn our heads to see the objects more directly in that low light, they become less visible, disappear even. For me as a writer, staring directly into that dim light, attempting to see the story before me, is futile. By viewing things on the peripheral of the non-contemplated, I can use my writer's vision to observe otherwise undetected motion. But we must wait for that peripheral glimpse, be ready for it to appear, and know that even then its clarity will be compromised because of, and in spite of, the words.

The story idea I was contemplating while at that *Strassenbahn* stop involved an experience earlier in the day. I had been on my way to class, walking down the stairs from my sixth-floor office. On the landing to the fifth floor, I passed some workers refurbishing an office. From a paint-splattered portable radio standing on the floor, Fleetwood Mac sang "You can go your own way, go your own way." Not only would the GDR state have found the message unacceptable, but also that the lyrics were in English. And yet now at least half the songs on pop radio stations here are sung in English. Still, if I walked up to the workers and started speaking in my native tongue, we would probably exhaust our conversation after some greetings and small talk about the weather. We could probably get a little further if we spoke German, but I wasn't planning to ask whether the workers thought Stevie Nicks has a voice like a snake charmer or just a snake. And because my German isn't good enough to get into any in-depth discussions about those things people should avoid—religion, sex, politics—we would have been better off just singing some pop songs together. At least we might all know the words.

As I considered this, I decided to make a note of the scene. I was standing at the top of a wide staircase heading to the landing between the fourth and fifth floors. I began to step while writing. My foot reached out and found nothing but air. Instead of continuing to shift my weight forward, I pulled back. I looked down to see that I had misjudged the distance to the next stair. I exhaled in relief as I thought of how close I came to tumbling down the staircase and having the workers rush down to check on me. I was less worried about the pain than the ensuing conversation, our common vocabulary based in song lyrics. How would they react to a fallen man who couldn't communicate well with them? Might they say, "This is not your stairway to heaven"? Would I respond "Whoa-oa-oa! I feel good, I knew that I would, now"? What if an ambulance and medical technicians were summoned? How does one say "broken ankle" in German? Or use it in a sentence, as in: "If I didn't have a broken ankle, I could give myself that kick in the ass I deserve for not learning German better"?

With the sun pushing low across the sky and me trying to form these questions and situations into a story, the streetcar pulled up and I got on, careful to step over the gap between car and platform.

It's ironic that in just over a decade-long stretch, I spent three years living in Germany. I have no Germanic heritage. I was never particularly interested in Germany. I knew little about the country. I am not a history enthusiast. When I announced that I planned to move to Germany the first time, my mother pursed her lips tightly then said, "Your grandfather hated the Germans." I had not known this and she had not thought it relevant enough to share this with me before then. As an air raid warden during World War II, he patrolled their small farming town in the middle of Michigan's thumb—a non-target if ever there was one—verifying that his neighbors pulled tight their shades and curtains so no light could escape and be spotted by the nonexistent German bombers flying overhead. "He took this position," my mother told me, "very seriously."

Nor did I study the language, though I had considered it in college. Instead, I followed someone's advice to take French because its nouns only had two genders rather than German's three. Even then, I struggled with the language requirement, at a time when my cognitive ability to learn a language was supposedly much better than it was when I first went to Germany a decade later.

When I left for Giessen, I didn't know more than a handful of words. I twice started courses offered by the city, but bored with the routine and my lack of progress, I quit. Being in a department of English also allowed me to neglect my German. I could almost always find someone to speak English with. A couple of the secretaries didn't know or weren't comfortable enough with the language to speak it, but in our delimited German conversations, we always managed.

My reluctance to speak German was exacerbated by my students, who were studying English as a foreign language. They could not pass up the opportunity to interact with a native speaker, especially an American, as most Germans who teach English are trained in British English. Yet, in the German university system where students do not officially register for classes, I noted a precipitous drop-off after the third week of each semester. Thinking students didn't like my class, I brought this up with a colleague. She assured me that from the beginning these students had no intention of staying. They came to hear my accent, to pick up the sounds and intonations of an American. Once they thought they had heard enough, they simply stopped coming.

And in the west of Germany, one could get away with switching into English during an emergency situation—say someone falling down a flight of stairs—because almost all have studied the language. Many westerners will claim not to speak English well, yet they will then break into almost unaccented English. At the very least, most everyone speaks some version of passable English. In the former East, speaking English during that emergency might very well have brought forth nothing more than blank stares.

People who considered their English to be pretty good said things like "please" after you have said "thank you" because in German the word for "please" and "you're welcome"—*bitte*—are one and the same. Of course, English was not the primary foreign language taught in East German schools. Russian was. If a GDR student wanted to learn English, he or she could take it as a third or fourth language. There were situations where, from the government's perspective, having citizens know English was advantageous, spy work among them. Yet, paradoxically, wanting to learn English brought suspicion on those who chose to study it. A potential defector, no doubt.

While I have described my German as "almost functional," I might more accurately describe it as "department store." To people who ask, I say my German is "immer beschissen," always shitty. I can participate in situational conversations. I can sometimes even wander a short way from these. But remove me from these formulaic situations and, like a dog on a leash, I eventually run out of line and find myself choking without the vocabulary to go further, links in the chain I could install myself if I were more capable. My grasp of the language remains limited. I am sad to say this, but I admit my failings. I enjoy the country; I love the people; but I cannot overcome the language.

Not knowing German well, I cannot look Germany square in the face. I cannot participate in the society the way someone who is fluent in the language can. The inability to communicate my thoughts and ideas in any language is frustrating. As I sit here at my computer deleting, rearranging, and restarting, this piece serves as an example. When writing, though, I can always stop. The paper is my conversation partner, but it doesn't talk back much. With German, my language ability is so limited that my exasperation is constant. This leads to continual conflict between my desire to interact and my fear of leaving the safety of silence, where I will be forced to speak and cannot simply shrug off or ignore what was said. Yet sometimes we observers become witnesses, participants in the milieu of lives we have chosen but not anticipated.

The *Fulbright Primer*, a booklet provided by the German-American Fulbright Commission, emphasizes the need to become as fluent as possible. The *Primer* states that "an excellent knowledge of the German language is the key to a successful exchange experience . . . as well as for avoiding difficulties in your daily social contacts." Roberta and I worried less about missing out and more about the fear of something happening that our limited German would not allow us to cope with.

A lack of language facility means that any exchange can become problematic. Every conversation in German requires exertion, the piecing together of context and misunderstood words. When the phone rang in our apartment Roberta and I would stare at each other, hoping the other would volunteer to answer. Talking on a phone provides no contextual clues for deciphering words, no opportunity to point or gesture, and no possibility to make or read facial expressions. It does, however, provide plenty of opportunities for silence as one translates and formulates words. In the radio world, it is much more desirable to play very bad music or provide boring conversations and inane commentary than to have dead air. In silence, no one knows you exist. Stopping to contemplate what to say or how to say something during a phone conversation is the equivalent of dead air. Such silence can seem to the person on the other end as a lack of consideration, rudeness even. And the ensuing embarrassment can make one want to hang up the phone, a decisive action to halt the mortification.

One time, I got up my courage to call our friends Thomas and Evy Damm. They had loaned us some winter clothes while we awaited the arrival of a lost box we had shipped from the United States. The night prior I had left one of their hats at a restaurant when we were out together. I wasn't about to call the restaurant myself. That would require too much bravado on my part. Instead I rehearsed my lines and dialed the phone. Evy answered. Eastern-born, she speaks very little English.

"Hallo, hier ist Sandy."

"Ah, hallo. Wie geht's?"

"Ja, gut. Aber ich habe meine Mütze verloren."

"Wie bitte?"

"Ich habe meine Mütze verloren. Als wir gestern Abend zusammen waren, habe ich meine Mütze verloren."

"Wie?"

"Ich habe . . ."

"Vielleicht willst du mit Thomas sprechen?"

"Nein, ich will mit dir sprechen."

"Okay, aber was ist verloren?"

"Meine Mütze."

"Ach . . . hier ist Thomas."

For several seconds, a muffled discussion.

"Hello, Sandy. Now what's all this about?" Thomas asked. He was West German, and though he had spent a year in the United States, his accent was that of the British English he had been taught in school. I followed Thomas into the comfort of English.

"Last night, when we went out together, I lost the hat you gave me."

"The hat?"

"Yeah, the hat. Meine Mütze. That's what I was telling Evy."

The laughter began. He covered the phone again as he spoke to Evy. Barely controlling himself, he got back on the line.

"Oh, Evy thought you were saying 'meine Mutti.' She couldn't understand how you had lost your mother. Don't worry about the hat. It didn't cost much. We'll get another one."

While Thomas and Evy chuckled over my missing mother, I was crestfallen by my ineptitude. That Thomas was not worried about the hat—a Russian *ushanka* with large, detachable earflaps that I was fond of—made me even more disappointed for having spent so much energy planning the phone call.

My miscommunication with Evy portended a sleepless night. The closest I come to a recurring nightmare concerns my being in a band. In these dreams, I am convinced by others to perform on stage during a concert even though I tell everyone I don't really know how to play the instrument, usually a guitar. I start off well enough, able to stay with the band for a few bars. But I quickly reach my limits and end up standing there in front of the crowd, awkwardly trying to fake my way through fingering not only the rest of the song but the whole set. When I am in Germany, this fear over lack of preparation and competence addles me into sleepless nights where I rehearse conversational sets in German. I think about what I should have said during a discussion that day or imagine the next day's situations and what sorts of words I might need to draw on. Certainly, I would replay my rehearsed conversation with Evy over and over as I tossed through sleeplessness.

I often worried about other situations, too. What if I simply couldn't understand what someone who approached me said? What if I had to report a crime? What if someone collapsed in front of me? These are not rhetorical questions. Each of these happened to me during our stay in Erfurt. The last one occurred one day while riding the streetcar into work. As it slowed at the stop prior to the university, an elderly man lay on the tracks that were headed in the opposite direction. He was on his side, half curled up. No emergency vehicles had arrived. A few people, including the driver of the streetcar near him, hovered over the man. One bent to comfort or perhaps question him. Here, the tracks ran down a center median strip, so one would have to cross traffic to reach the platform. Perhaps the man had been struck by the streetcar as he moved in front of it. Or he could have fallen while trying to catch up to it before it left the stop. Maybe a car struck him as he crossed the road. I wondered if I would have witnessed the scene had I been on the previous streetcar. What would I have done? Gotten off and told the authorities I had seen it? "Ich habe das gesehen, aber mein Deutsch ist nicht so gut." I saw that, but my German isn't very good. It would be a start. But the start to what?

Later in our stay, but always with our language phobia at the forefront of our minds, Roberta and I left our apartment on our way to the store. Another elderly man, whose path we were crossing, grabbed at his chest and started heaving loudly. More questions: Was he choking? Having a heart attack? Was it an advanced case of emphysema? The man paused for a moment as we kept walking, but I turned back several times just to be sure. The man finally continued on his way. I looked back no more. If he had another attack, he was someone else's responsibility.

Another question, this one asked of me while still in Regensburg. The reporter's query had been straightforward enough: "What was your motivation for coming to Germany?" The woman worked for a Bavarian television station doing a story on American Fulbright recipients who were taking the intensive language course. I stood before the television camera and stated something about getting exposure to new cultures, visiting new places, meeting new people. I might as well have added "Be all you that you can be" since I sounded like an army recruiting ad.

Language, as it would so many times over the next year, failed me. Here is something closer to what I wanted to say:

> I believe that people must occasionally put themselves in a position where the comfort zone we spend so much of our lives trying to attain, and then maintain, is erased, where one is forced—because of the circumstances—to learn all over again. I believe that, at some point, we all stand at the threshold of the unknown and look into the room of fears. Some of us have no choice but to undertake such situations. Others of us—the more fortunate, like myself—have options and so get to choose the circumstances for this, allowing us to prepare for the experience. Perhaps it is unfair, but we could, under the most dire of circumstances, bail out and return to our lives. However, this doesn't make the unknown any more known as we confront it.

I didn't say this. I didn't have the ability to get the point across in German—nor very well in English, for that matter. Still, I wanted to say something, so I came up with my army-like slogan. Even the television people—purveyors of the sound bite—recognized the inanity of my response and edited me out of the broadcast.

After the ten-minute ride out to the *Plattenbau* district at the north end of town, I stopped by our apartment, as it was on the way to Callan's kindergarten. Since I would have to pass within five feet of our building's front door, I decided to drop off the heavy pack I was toting.

Ours was not the best area. In the United States we might call it a transition neighborhood. But this one was transitioning for the worse. Many of the *Plattenbau* were to be demolished under reunification, so little was being done to maintain those slated for demolition. These unintentional monuments to communism were being dismantled. People who lived in them knew they would have to move out soon or were only temporary tenants waiting to find another place. The generally run-down condition of the buildings was reflected in the behavior of some of the residents. One young man spent weekends on the ledge of his bedroom window catcalling to women walking below. After a raucous New Year's evening filled with firecrackers and fireworks as far as the eye could see, we awoke the next morning to find a window in the apartment's entryway door blown out, the black spray of gunpowder testifying to the explosive force that caused it.

Because many *Plattenbau* were in such bad shape, they often housed new immigrants to the former East, poor foreigners whose presence was often not wanted and who became scapegoats for the economic hardships facing easterners. Graffiti splayed across buildings, some of it espousing Nazi ideology. Other messages were harder to interpret. In the building adjoining ours, a sign was posted in a third-floor window. It read in handwritten letters "Böhse Onkelz," or "evil uncles," the name of a popular band that was originally associated with the neo-Nazi skinhead movement but whose lyrics shifted away from outright hatred to a more modest anger found in many bands. Thus, one wonders if the young man—it is most likely a young male—who faced this sign toward the street was just letting everyone know that he was a fan of the band, or if he was sending a warning to foreigners. A student at the university once brought me a website printout of a map showing those areas most densely populated by foreigners in eastern Germany. It was used, she told me, by skinheads and other anti-foreign groups to know where to focus their energies. Erfurt was among those highlighted.

I dropped my backpack in the entryway and stepped into the living room of our second-floor apartment to take a quick glance at the local newspaper, which, despite our never having order it, arrived daily. I thought I heard what sounded like young people yelling in the entrance foyer where the fireworks had exploded a floor below. But kids often sound like they're crying out in fear when they are playing, and so I tried to put it out of my mind. The noise continued to rise up from below. I couldn't hide in here; I needed to get Callan. I put on my jacket, closed the apartment door behind me, and walked down the stairs. Outside the window panes of the door, boys were shouting at one another. I walked into the middle of it before it escalated.

One boy stood inside the wind-protecting alcove, back against a wall, as I pulled the door open. He was two heads shorter than me with red hair and pale features. A few feet away stood another boy, at least as tall as me but heavier and probably older than the redhead. Though he was somewhat light skinned, many of his features—the kinky hair, the broad nose—were clearly African. Blacks in Germany are often referred to simply as "Afrikaner" since so many are recent immigrants from African nations and are trying to find a safer and better life in the former German Democratic Republic. But Germany is an insular society, and immigrants—despite numbering some ten million—face difficulty obtaining citizenship and an even harder time integrating into the society. African German then seems a descriptor that does not fit. So how to describe this young man-child? The label is unimportant, but the differences it delineates lay at the root of the encounter.

The large African boy was shouting something at the smaller white boy when I opened the door. He was flanked by two smaller white boys. One of them held a soccer ball in his arms. Given the size difference of the combatants, their assistance seemed unnecessary. Rather, they were probably serving as witnesses who would help support and perhaps embellish the African boy's later recounting of the tale.

As I walked into the middle of this, I acted as if I didn't know there was a problem. But there were two: theirs and mine. My *What should I say?* could not remain hypothetical for much longer. I turned to the white boy, anticipating more cooperation from the one who seemed most in need of help. Pink and red splotched his face. He had a scrape on one cheek. Under his eyes, a puffiness. I couldn't tell whether it came from crying—he clearly had been despite what seemed his intention not to—or whether he had been struck in both eyes and they were on their way to becoming swollen. Upon closer examination, I suspected both.

"What's going on?" I asked him in German. He shrugged. His breathing was hard and adrenalin-filled. I didn't recognize him, but since he was in the alcove, I thought he might be from our building.

"Where do you live?" I asked him.

"Baumerstrasse," he answered. The street was beyond the university, a fifteen-minute *Strassenbahn* ride away.

"Who is that?" I asked him, pointing at the larger boy.

"Er ist Neger," he replied.

At least that is what I think he said. I did not expect to

hear this from him, nor had I ever heard the term used before. I couldn't be sure whether *Neger* was a German equivalent of the derogatory term, even with its different pronunciation so that it came out something like "nay-ger." What if *Neger* was a common and acceptable term here? What if I had misheard and he used the more derogatory term?

"Was hat er gesagt?" the tall boy asked one of his comrades. What did he say? He grabbed the soccer ball and bounced it hard against the ground.

One of them told him. I listened carefully; this time I was more sure of the word used. The dark-skinned boy tossed his head slightly. He bounced the ball again.

I turned back to the white boy. I stared, wondering what to say next. I was shocked that he was so emboldened that, even after having taken what appeared to be a beating, he was still willing to stick to his racist statements. Perhaps he was now hiding behind me, somehow believing that I would become his ally, that I too would support his bigotry toward the older boy. After all, I was a fortyish white man living in a *Plattenbau.*

Had I been able to scold him in German, I'm not sure I would have done so. I once owned a button with a photo of two young boys, one black and one white, their arms around one another. Below were the words "No one is born a bigot." The unlearning of racist tendencies could not be undone with a simple reprimand. Even if our conversation were being conducted in English, I might have been at a loss for words.

But I was not even sure that I heard what I thought I heard. Maybe he had said something completely different, and it was I who had imposed race onto the discussion. I looked into his green eyes, swollen with fear—or was it defiance?

"Weg," I commanded finally. Go away.

He hesitated, as if about to say something, then took off running, rounded the corner and disappeared. At least he didn't head toward the apartment with the Böhse Onkelz sign.

The dark-skinned boy bounced the ball once more then kicked it against the side of the building so that it ricocheted off in the direction the other had gone. He started to chase after it, but I moved alongside him, keeping myself between him and his route to the red-haired boy.

"You stay here," I said in German.

"Yeah, okay," he replied. "I'm staying here."

He picked up the ball and began to walk back toward his friends, bouncing it against the cement again.

"He's a little small, isn't he?" I asked the bigger boy in German.

"What?" he said, as if he didn't understand me, as if to remind me that I was the foreigner here.

I repeated myself.

"Yeah, yeah. He's a little small," he agreed.

"And you're a little big, no?" I was stalling for time.

"Yeah, yeah," he mumbled.

I had nothing more to say. He bounced the ball some more. We stood in silence for a long time.

Finally, the three remaining boys began to meander toward the corner around which the red-haired boy had disappeared. I let them go. I figured I had given him enough of a head start.

A few months after the encounter with the boys, I stood on Domplatz watching the Fasching parade. The Carnival-like extravaganza includes gaudily dressed participants tossing candy to youngsters and condoms to teens and handing out small bottles of schnapps to the adults. As I watched a float pass by, I glimpsed out of the corner of my eye the red-haired boy only a few people away. His physical bruises had healed, though he seemed even smaller among the crowd. He stood between his parents, who smiled as they watched their son call out for the revelers to throw him candy. They chortled when he caught something. I had spent many restless nights replaying that alcove confrontation in my head. I wanted to walk over and scold the boy, then warn his parents about the child they were raising. Or maybe scold them too—for the child they were raising.

Long after I stood in front of that German TV camera, I realized that the reporter had asked the right question and I had given the right answer. It may be a cliché, but I came to Germany to be all that I could be. I wanted to live up to the potential within me. In the end, I learned where my limits lay. I became not the person I had hoped to be—in that, I fell short—but the person my words allowed me to become.

7. Destinations and Wanderings

Haltestelle: Thüringen-Park

The block-long walk from our apartment to the streetcar stop, or *Haltestelle*, at Thüringen-Park mall took us past a row of *Plattenbau*. It was common not only here but throughout this apartment-filled city to see people—retirees, the unemployed, the curious and bored—leaning out their open windows, even in winter, watching the world pass by. Many did it for such long stretches that they rested their arms against pillows placed on the ledge. EVAG, Erfurt's public transportation company, appealed to the sedentary by adorning some streetcars with the slogan *Fensterplätze für Erfurt: Die Stadtbahn auf 6 Linien, 72 kms*. In other words, EVAG's six lines covering about forty-five miles offered riders window seats on the city. Why sit in an apartment window and watch the world go by, the ad implied, when taking the streetcar allows one to travel past all of Erfurt?

Though the mobile billboards didn't persuade us, once the Escort was stolen and our landlords understandably decided fixing the car wasn't worth it, these streetcars became our window seats on Erfurt, our way of seeing the city's offerings. The Number 3 line ran from Ulan-Bator-Strasse at the north end, one stop beyond ours, to Windischholzhausen, south of town. The line followed Nordhäuser strasse south, where it becomes Andreasstrasse as it reaches the old part of the city. We normally rode only as far as the center of town, usually getting off at Domplatz or sometimes even Anger, where half a dozen tracks asterisk in the center of the large, pedestrian-friendly shopping district.

Even though ours was one of Erfurt's last areas to be built up, we were provided the oldest streetcars—perhaps an attempt to keep housing and transportation in the same era. Unlike the sleek, quiet, spacious cars of recent vintage with their automated voices announcing the *nächste Haltestelle*, LED signs, and flooring level with the platform, ours were loud, wobbly, and required three steps up to board. And instead of an electronic beep to warn passengers that the doors were closing, our cars clanged a bell that reminded me of my regimented elementary school years. So too did some of the passengers.

One day, we joined our *Plattenbau* neighbors and a few mall shoppers on the streetcar platform. Callan was feeling particularly energetic. She darted between people and called to us, hoping we would chase her. On the platform, a thick, painted line ran about a foot and a half from the concrete edge nearest the track and parallel to it. Those waiting to board were expected to stand behind this, keeping a safe distance from the drop-off. Callan dashed about the platform, her purple jacket and scarf flying behind her. She didn't notice an elderly bystander who kept watch, pretending to be disinterested. But as soon as Callan put one foot onto the yellow line, the woman scolded Callan for not being careful, shaking a finger in her direction. And for good measure, she turned and reprimanded us for allowing our child to run wild, finger still wagging. Such societal pressure to ensure that others are following rules is common in Germany. People there are, I believe, less likely to look the other way. Yet, the strict interpretation of the rules—Callan's toes touching the line—can be disconcerting. I said, "Ja, ja" to the woman, thanked her for her concern, and in English asked Callan not to anger the woman again. Callan the indomitable continued to dart around the platform, avoiding the line.

Nächste Haltestelle: Bergstrasse

One fall afternoon we rode south on our usual route, passing Strasse der Nationen, Warschauer strasse, Reithstrasse, Donaustrasse, Klinikum/Universität (my stop for work), and Baumerstrasse. As we approached Bergstrasse, the sun was already setting over the horizon to our right. A man stood up and walked to the front of the wagon. He was not old, fifty at most, but it was clear life had not been kind to him. His body was nothing more than a hanger for his clothes, which appeared to have spent much time in a heap. The man's face was as wrinkled as his clothes. Even from a distance, he appeared to be a little out of his head, a bit *Verrückt*, as one might say in German, while waving a hand, palm inward, in front of one's face. As he stood at the front waiting for the wagon to come to a halt, he reached his right arm upward. At first I thought he was giving the Nazi salute, but that seemed impossible. More likely, he was grasping for the overhead bar to steady himself but not quite reaching it. When his hand remained up, not holding onto anything, I again suspected he was saluting. I couldn't even begin to imagine what had caused the man to be attracted to neo-Nazism at an age far beyond when most disaffected youth would. Yet I felt simultaneously guilty for my own unseemly conjecturing. I turned to Roberta. She shrugged, also unsure of what she was seeing.

At Bergstrasse, the man careened down the stairs, mumbling to himself. I turned around as the streetcar began to pull away. The man still stood in the road facing us, his posture stiff. He brought his legs together and clicked his heels, right arm at a forty-five degree angle, palm flat, saluting us. The man's image became smaller and smaller as we rode off along the sunset.

Nächste Haltestelle: Domplatz

On December 23, the streetcar squealed to a halt at Domplatz and we disembarked into the year's first bitterly cold day. This area below the hilltop cathedral and church hosts the annual *Weihnachtsmarkt*, an open-air fair filled with chalet-style huts that lasts from late November until a few days before Christmas. The *Weihnachtsmarkt* offers visitors the chance to buy Christmas gifts and ornaments, go on carnival rides, eat various kinds of food, including roasted chestnuts and bowls of sautéed mushrooms, and share a glass of mulled wine, *Glühwein*, with friends. Many cities and villages in Germany host a *Weihnachtsmarkt* with their almost-too-perfect holiday atmosphere. No matter how large the city, the *Weihnachtsmarkt* suggests a picturesque small-town atmosphere, though my image of them is sullied by once having seen in Frankfurt a very thin Santa Claus drinking a beer and smoking a cigarette during his midmorning break.

We had already visited Erfurt's market once, but we returned on this day to meet up with Thomas and Evy Damm and their children and to close down the market for the season. Both Thomas and Evy are professionals: he a lawyer and she a bridge engineer for Deutsche Bahn, the German railroad company. Because of our varying language abilities, somebody missed out on part of any untranslated conversation. But we enjoyed their company because they liked to eat, drink, and laugh. As importantly, they had two daughters near in age to ours. Marlene, nine at the time, coupled riveting blue eyes with a subdued demeanor that made her seem much more adult than her years. Clara, a diminutive for Clarissa, was five and had blond hair the color of Callan's but cut a bit shorter. The two were sometimes confused for sisters because Clara's rambunctiousness, exuberance, and defiant ways equaled Callan's.

We met thanks to one of Roberta's moments of bravery. A month before, Roberta took Callan to an *Auslander Gesellschaft Tag*, a daylong opportunity to learn about foreign people and cultures. This was held at Engelsburg, one of the oldest stone houses in Germany, dating to the early twelfth century, but which is now part of a student center for the university. Because Callan and a girl who turned out to be Clara were having a good deal of fun playing together, Roberta decided she should introduce herself to the mother. Roberta managed to hold a conversation in German with Evy, and the two exchanged contact information.

The five o'clock closing on that December day marked the end of the *Weihnachtsmarkt* season. Our agreed-upon goal for the afternoon was to finish off the large vats of *Glühwein* at our chosen hut. We tried, toasting each new drink until the market shut down. In the numbing cold, we kept our hands warm by wrapping them around mugs filled with the heated wine. Yet we also wanted to warm our insides with wine, so we continually drank, emptied, and needed to refill.

When one drinks at a *Glühwein* hut, normally one pays a *Pfand*, or a small deposit, on the coffee-sized mugs the mulled wine is served in. The deposit ensures that hut owners don't lose money on those who wander off with drink in hand. But we hadn't paid the *Pfand* because Evy assured the server we weren't going anywhere and would be standing at one of the high tables only a few yards away.

As we tipped back the last of our *Glühwein* and reined in

the girls, Evy insisted that we needed souvenirs to take back to the U.S. She tried to convince me to steal the mugs, which are decorated with a painted version of the *Weihnachtsmarkt* scene we stood within. I declined several times. Evy told me to drop them in the big pockets of my jacket. No one would see, she said. I acquiesced only when Thomas agreed to serve pro bono as my attorney were I to get caught and hauled off to the police station, though I knew the police were probably too busy to bother with such a "crime."

Nächste Haltestelle: Puschkinstrasse

In February, we rode the 3 line to Anger and transferred over to the 5, which we rode to Puschkinstrasse in a southwestern portion of the city we had never visited before. Here, large apartment buildings built before the war crowded together, filling city blocks, with a few bakeries and other small stores on corners. We disembarked from the streetcar, walked two blocks to the apartment building we had been provided the directions for, found the name Damm on a tag next to a doorbell, and pushed the buzzer.

A voice from the intercom sang, "Eine Minute!" We waited a while, and just when we were about to ring again, Marlene and Clara opened the apartment building door and welcomed us.

The girls escorted us upstairs past three floors of landings, each with doors leading into apartments and an arrangement of small tables, rugs, pictures, and knick-knacks that individualized the common areas. On the top floor, there was only one door, which led into the Damms' apartment. We walked directly into the living room. Low couches and chairs were covered in white twill. A three-foot-high candelabra stood off to the side. A woman's face as tall as the candelabra filled a canvas leaning against one wall.

Evy and Thomas emerged from the kitchen, Thomas wiping his hands on a towel. While he finished packing up some foodstuffs, Evy showed us around the apartment. Though most rooms had pitched ceilings, the apartment was bigger than our house in Jersey. In the large kitchen, a chrome refrigerator with a rounded front was surrounded by frosted-glass cupboards. The bedrooms all had more floor space than any of ours back home. Even the bathroom was spacious, four or five times the size of ours in the *Plattenbau*. At one end of the living room a set of large sliding doors opened onto a balcony. We walked out and saw other apartments and a few trees. Even this high up, the view was that of a city.

Since their feet touched earth only when they left their apartment, the Damms rented a *Schrebergarten*, a small plot of land on the outskirts of town. We understood from Roberta's making plans on the phone with Evy that we would meet at their apartment then walk to the *Schrebergarten*. As we toured the apartment, Thomas took the supplies downstairs, including a large basket filled with picnic items we had brought. He would deliver them to the garden house while we walked to the Waldkasino, a restaurant near their apartment, where we would meet up with him and another couple. From there, we were told, we would hike to the *Schrebergarten*.

The Waldkasino, once a functioning casino, now is a restaurant and beer garden located at the edge of the Steigerwald, a somewhat hilly seventeen-hundred-acre preserve just south of town. The groomed trails running through the woods typify the German approach to nature—beautiful but tamed by man.

After the group had gathered in the Waldkasino parking lot, we began walking. And walked. And walked some more. Fortunately, the mid-February weather was a moderate forty-five degrees. Eventually we reached the appropriately named Waldhaus, "house in the woods." Under the same ownership as the Waldkasino, this Victorian-style brick building with clipped gables felt like a fairy tale find. Inside, vaulted ceilings and half-timber framing above wooden tables and large windows looking out on the forest gave the restaurant a sense of *Gemutlichkeit*, or coziness. While the adults drank beer brewed on the premises, the kids ate large ice cream concoctions that are a staple throughout Germany. Fortified, we left the Waldhaus and began walking again. We alternated between skirting the wood's edge and walking through well-tended paths surrounded by trees.

The hiking continued. There was no garden in sight. By now it was close to 3:30, and Roberta dropped back to where Callan and I were bringing up the rear. "I thought Evy had said they had something to do tonight. Did I misunderstand somehow?" she asked.

Although Thomas was at the front of the group that had by now spread out across fifty yards, he turned around and declared, as if overhearing us, "We are still a ways from the garden house. At least an hour."

I thought he was kidding. Then we stopped. Evy removed the backpack she had been carrying and unzipped it, pulling out a picnic: cheeses, crackers, knives, napkins. Roberta shot me a glance that showed her irritation. The picnic food we brought to share was sitting at the garden house, wherever that was. After we enjoyed the snacks, Evy reached into the backpack and pulled out small, airline-sized bottles of Aromatique, a schnapps popular in the east, which she passed out to the adults. When we finished, we packed up and pressed onward.

While Tara and I were walking apart from the adults at the front and the kids at the back, she confided, "I can't believe we wasted the whole day walking." I explained to her that this was a common German form of light exercise. *Wandern* often means a long walk with a destination in mind yet without necessarily taking the shortest route to reach it: purposeful wandering.

As promised by Thomas, almost an hour later we surmounted a hill. Below us stood a *Schrebergartenanlage*, a grouping of perhaps four dozen huts with small paths connecting them. It was nearing five. We had been hiking almost three hours. Nearby stood Thüringenhalle, a concert venue that is no more than a ten-minute walk from the Damm's apartment. We had nearly completed our wandering circle.

These *Schrebergarten* are city-owned, community-style gardens. People rent a small plot of land at a reasonable rate and build a little cabin-style hut on it. Since so many Germans live in apartments, this provides city dwellers a piece of earth in which to dig, plant, and enjoy the outdoors. Some places are quite fancy, more like cottages, and people might spend the whole summer living in these garden houses. In the Damm's *Schrebergartenanlage* all of the cabins have electricity, running water, and toilets, even though the latter are technically illegal. Because so much of Germany was bombed during World War II, many people were forced to live in their garden houses, some for years. The Damm's plot was about the size of our back yard in Jersey. Two terraced rectangles were reserved for vegetables and herbs. Two apple trees, a peach tree, and a large pine tree also stood in the yard. Thorned rose stems and other remains from onceflowering plants decorated the front of the hut. Inside, unfinished walls and spare furnishing promised nothing more than they offered. Only the lace curtains provided any hint at opulence. The previous owner built the hut during GDR times, and Thomas said that no doubt most of the materials were stolen from the local company the man worked for, as materials were otherwise hard to come by.

Apparently, the Damms had no appointment since we stayed there until well after nine, grilling brats and chatting. Nothing much happened on that uneventful evening at the garden hut. But as the Damms and their friends talked to one another in German about the mad cow scare, children, and the day's walk, I did not need to follow every word to know we were being permitted to glimpse a normal evening with these Germans, an evening not unlike many I have spent with my own friends. Seven months into our year abroad, such normalcy was enough for me.

Nächste Haltestelle: Reith

Late at night when fewer streetcars are needed, our Number 3 combined with the Number 6, a second line that ran the same route as 3 out of town but then made a right-hand turn toward Reith, an area where Tara's school was located. This combination route, called the N3, or what we referred to as the "night train," moved north until turning right, toward Reith. It then circled back to the same intersection and resumed the trip northward to our Thüringen-Park stop at the mall.

One Tuesday evening, Roberta and I left the kids behind and rode into town to see a blues musician. We returned around 10:30, late enough for the night train. We were never sure whether it was because of the Reith area or that we were riding the night train, but though it traveled only a little bit out of the way, the night train always seemed to pick up passengers from all walks of limping life.

A couple of stops into the trip on this particular night, a man staggered aboard. I saw him out of the corner of my eye and figured he was drunk. He walked in our direction and stopped to hold onto a pole nearby, providing me a better look. Over his right eyebrow ran a gash that was at least two inches in length. Worse, it swelled out at least another inch. Blood had flowed out of the open wound, pooled in the man's eyebrow, and run down into his swollen right eye. When he turned, the whole right side of his face, including the left eye, that half of his nose, and his cheek, were a bruised mottling of deep black, blue, and even green. The man somehow managed to stay upright, swaying with the car. A few stops later, he staggered off and began to head purposefully in the direction of a *Plattenbau*.

Endhaltestelle: Steigerstrasse

In June, Germans celebrate the Ascension, known as Cristi Himmelfahrt, or as I prefer to literally translate it, "Christ's drive to heaven." It also turned out to be what we would consider Father's Day. We decided to have a family picnic in the Steigerwald, and by late morning we had packed our backpacks, taken the Number 3 to Anger, transferred to the 5, ridden that to the end, and hiked into the woods.

A little way in, we began to hear cheers going up throughout the woods. We thought it was coming from a soccer match. As we walked on, we encountered a group of men sitting on some benches atop a hill. They were chanting something, but I couldn't make it out, so I asked Tara.

"I can't tell what they're saying, but I can tell you they're drunk," she said.

I chortled at her disparaging comment. As we walked on, we encountered more groups of men ranging from small clusters of three or four to fifteen or more. Some were talking, others were singing, many were cheering: all were drinking. We couldn't find anywhere without people, so we sat down by a pond to unpack our bread, salami, and pears beneath a crowd that had taken over a small structure on the ridge above us. They called to anyone walking by on the path, blaring their horns and toasting everything.

After lunching, we headed to the Waldhaus we had last visited with the Damms to try out their *Biergarten* for the first time. As we drew nearer, the noise and singing increased. When we rounded the corner, we encountered hundreds of people, almost all men, gathered around rows of picnic tables. Some of the younger ones drank from beer bongs. Here and there, a group played cards. Most drank, talked, and sang, with others joining each new song. I looked at my watch: 1:00 p.m.

We sat at a table apart from the other groups on the very edge of the festivities. Nearby, on a kids' inflatable, bouncy castle, a man had passed out. A few small boys jumped nearby, flopping him to and fro each time they landed. In the other direction, two men stood and raised their fists to one another. One of them, a tall man with hair down to the middle of his back, called a time-out to put it in a ponytail, then knocked the other man to the ground with one punch. He then helped up his fallen opponent, shook his hand, and both went back to drinking. Catcalls and whistles rained down on any unaccompanied woman who walked by, including one who arrived with what appeared to be her sister and mother, and for some reason wore the most clingy black dress she could pour herself into. When Roberta went to the bathroom, she too was catcalled. Later, when we were about to leave and she went again, Roberta took Callan with her. She received stares, she reported, but no one said anything to or about her.

So while Americans would spend Father's Day celebrating their fatherhood with their family, we found that eastern German men spend it escaping the family. No wonder the day is also known as Männertag, or, in the east, Herrentag, "Men's Day."

Endhaltestelle: Ulan-Bator-Strasse

Heading north toward home required taking the Number 3 toward Ulan-Bator-Strasse, the last stop. Early in our stay, after we explored some new areas of town, we rode the streetcar past Thüringen-Park and instead got off at Ulan Bator. This was just the next stop after ours, so we decided to take a leisurely walk back to our apartment. As we stepped off the streetcar into a new part of our neighborhood filled with even more apartment buildings, I realized how little of this large *Plattenbaugebiete*, or *Plattenbau* zone, we normally saw, since our building stood near the front of the large neighborhood.

We wandered among the *Plattenbau*, noting how people used flowers, wall hangings, and other decorations to individualize their balcony from the dozens of others facing the street. We eventually reached a small restaurant with outdoor seating that was not open, nor would it be any other time we attempted to visit.

Later, during a conversation with Manuela and Wilfried, I happened to mention our taking the *Strassenbahn* to Ulan Bator.

"We have been there," Manuela said, matter-of-factly.

"You've taken the *Strassenbahn* out past our place?" I asked.

"No, we've been to Ulan Bator. The one in Mongolia."

"Ja, ja. Nineteen hundred and seven..." Wilfried paused to reverse the numerals from the German way of saying them. Finally, he completed his thought: "eighty-seven." He grinned.

"Really?" Roberta asked.

"Do you have photos?" I exclaimed.

"No, only these." Wilfried held his finger together to make a small square. Slides. Wilfried went on to explain—Manuela filling in the English words he did not know—that near the end of GDR times getting a roll of 36-exposure film developed would cost 80 East German Marks, at a time when people made a lot less money. So they always had the much cheaper slides made.

Ulan Bator is almost five thousand miles from Germany, yet being the capital of communist Mongolia made it a destination for East Germans. Prior to the Wall's fall, Manuela served as a guide and translator for people visiting East Germany, but once a year she could serve the same role on a trip abroad. She was allowed a second ticket, which Wilfried's mother's purchased for his thirtieth birthday present. Wilfried and Manuela also got engaged a few days prior to departure, so this served not only as a working vacation but also as an impromptu engagement trip.

A week after our discussion, I received an e-mail invitation from Manuela with the subject line "Mongolian evening." We took the streetcar through the city to Arbeitsamt, the employment office and the stop nearest their house. Wilfried picked us up in their small station wagon and took us to their home in the woods, where we dined on a German version of pasties and cucumber soup with fresh dill, and of course lots of beer and wine. Afterward, Wilfried set up the projector and screen so we could view the slides from Ulan Bator and the other places they visited in Mongolia.

Many slides were from the Khangai Mountain region, a barren steppe where airplanes would land right on the grass. The photos were wonderful, the hues intensified. In one, Manuela stands in a *deel*, the traditional Mongolian herder outfit resembling a colorful caftan. Because Mongols are small people, only Manuela could fit into the photo-opportunity *deel*. It was also there that Manuela, Wilfried, and their East German traveling companions would discover the value of the U.S. dollar. Radeberger, brewed in Dresden, cost one East German mark in an Erfurt store in 1987. In the nomad's yurt—a round tent with a wooden door that also served as a bar—Radeberger was an import and cost seven and a half East German marks. Western beers were also available, but one had to purchase them using dollars, which they had none of.

While East German travel destinations were limited by a country's political affiliations, this was not so with West Germans, and they also touristed Mongolia as part of larger vacation packages. For them, Mongolia was just another stop; for Eastern bloc travelers, it was their destination. And whenever these Westerners needed a plane, the Easterners would get bumped in favor of those paying with the coveted dollars.

They also told us how out of the group of twenty-four, only two people were not a couple. The man, a gynecologist from Berlin, was the only one who seemed to enjoy nothing about the vacation. It did not take long to surmise that he was a Stasi agent assigned to keep an eye on the contingent, and he even admitted as much. Having constant contact with foreigners, Manuela was used to being observed. But when the group arrived at the Ulan Bator airport for departure, the wife of another doctor was pulled from the group for interrogation. She had made friends with some Austrians who were sharing their hotel deep in a Mongolian forest. Manuela, who served as the translator during the questioning, was shocked to find out that Mongolians were also watching them, even in such a remote area.

Our wonderment kept being interrupted by the slides sticking in the machine. Manuela explained the problem: "The pictures are East German; the machine is West German. They just don't get along."

Endhaltestelle: Europaplatz

When we visited Erfurt again in 2007, much about the city's public transportation system had changed. In the intervening half-dozen years, the rickety streetcars to our former neighborhood had been replaced by those gleaming, electronic marvels. All platforms now displayed the LED signs showing how many minutes remained until the next streetcar's arrival. New lines had been added. Old routes had been altered or extended as the city expanded its boundaries. And today *Haltestelle* Ulan-Bator-Strasse is no more. *Haltestelle* Europaplatz has replaced it. Same destination, different name.

In a 1991 visit to Budapest, two years after the Wall fell, I rented a room from an elderly woman who lived in a beautiful if slightly run-down apartment building on Erzsébet Körút, or Elizabeth Boulevard. The only language we shared was our equally bad German. My host knew enough to explain that when she moved into the apartment with her husband prior to World War II, the street was called Erzsébet and was very expensive to live on. After World War II and the communist takeover, the street was renamed Leninstrasse. The rent was very reasonable, so she was able to continue living there after her husband's death. Once the Wall fell, Erzsébet Körút returned, accompanied by a large increase in rent—forcing her to take in tourists.

In Erfurt, the Number 3 line probably didn't extend into what were farm fields until the *Plattenbau* were built by the communists in the 1970s, and thus the Ulan Bator stop didn't exist then either. But now Ulan Bator had become Europaplatz just as Leninstrasse in Budapest had become Erzsébet Körút.

People living on Erfurt's Number 3 line can no longer make Ulan Bator the street their destination, just as people living in the former GDR need no longer make Ulan Bator the city a destination. But those who have been to Ulan Bator—in streetcars and filmstrips—understand that destinations are only *vorübergehende Haltestellen*, temporary stops, during our imaginations' wanderings.

8. Field without Dreams
Baseball in the Former GDR

The game that seems to have inspired almost as many great quotes as it has spectacular catches once stirred Dizzy Dean to offer his solution to the Cold War: "I'd get me a bunch of bats and balls and sneak me a couple of umpires and learn them kids behind the Iron Curtain how to tote a bat and play baseball." Apparently, Dizzy felt this would show "them kids" how life was to be lived, how grand the American game—and thus American democracy—really was. Yet, it is "them kids" from whom our American youth could now learn a summer lesson.

One warm May day, we took a walk down to the large neighborhood park. These downtrodden *Plattenbau* make one yearn for the outdoors after a long winter. After four-year-old Callan had worn herself out climbing and swinging on playground equipment, we kept walking, taking a new route home through the other end of the park.

As we rounded a stand of large bushes, we heard shouting—not from surprise or fear—but calling out, calling back ... a pidgin version of baseball chatter: "Strike drei! Batter ist aus!" "Du bist safe!" Even "Pitcher hat einen Gummiarm!"

Before us stood a baseball field, a bit of America in the middle of the former German Democratic Republic. The diamond itself was regulation—I later paced off the distances from mound to home and home to first—with groomed base paths, batter's boxes, even on-deck circles and a fenced backstop. However, like the chatter, the players had adapted the game to fit their surroundings. The corner bases were moved a couple of yards toward the pitcher's mound; second had been eliminated. Scoring a run required running from "first" to "third" to home.

But even reaching base proved challenging. The batters' stances were awkward—one all elbows, another with feet too far apart. They swung, often and wildly, at most every pitch, no matter whether it crossed the plate or required a broom handle to reach it. There weren't enough gloves to go around; these were exchanged as the teams passed on the field. Indeed, there were barely enough players for one full team, let alone two. In addition to the pitcher and catcher, a couple of infielders and the random outfielder played their positions. Only a few in this ragtag assortment wore actual baseball caps—all embossed with the Yankees' logo. Still these youngsters, many of whom must have been born after the Wall fell, were, without a doubt, playing baseball.

When I was growing up, my knowledge of East German athletics focused every fourth year on the questionable genders of their Olympic swimmers. I didn't realize then that these superlative athletes received special privileges in the supposedly egalitarian communist country: the best apartments, cars provided without the decade-and-a-half-long waiting period, even vacations in Cuba. Perhaps, on such trips these athlete-celebrities first saw a Cuban baseball game and—unknown to Dizzy—sneaked it back behind the Iron Curtain. Or since all of Germany's professional baseball teams are located in the former West, perhaps the sport has been imported, like so much in what was once the GDR, from that part of the country.

Whatever the lineage, it was clear that this east German version of baseball differed from the cutthroat competitiveness so common in the way sports are played in America today. In our southern New Jersey neighborhood—and I am sure mine was typical of neighborhoods throughout the country—all the kids, ours included, were in leagues: baseball, softball, soccer, field hockey, youth football. Never once have they congregated for a game of pickup ball, even with large yards outside the door and sports fields within walking distance. Instead, American youth play only organized games under the often-judgmental gaze of adults, who seem to envision a potential big leaguer in every child.

Watching these young Germans adapt the game to their surroundings, I was reminded of the Michigan neighborhood of my youth and long days of two-man in the Herbers' backyard using taped wiffle bats and tennis balls scavenged from behind the municipal courts across the road. Since the area was surrounded by trees, the tennis players who hit shots over the fence would, like golfers, often lose their ball in the woods. A trip to the courts could net the four of us a bagful of balls. We would then return to the backyard with its eight-foot-high outfield fence and play fast pitch, leaving home runs in the neighboring yard of the Burns's, whose son was one of the players, until our supply ran out.

And I was reminded of days playing on a field tucked between the freeway and the Church of the Nazarene, whose modern, tentlike design included a large stained-glass front intersected by a wooden cross. One time, Danny Majeski hit a ball—a real baseball this time—farther than anyone had ever seen. As it headed toward the window, everyone turned. Stunned, we watched as it hit near the cross's intersection and bounced harmlessly into the bushes below—a home run that obviously not even Danny believed he had hit since he stood rooted to home plate, crossing himself in thanks for the unbroken glass.

It was during these times that my friends and I were snickering about the East German swimmers, whose gender seemed identifiable only by the suit they wore. We easily absorbed the American master narrative telling us that the free market capitalist economy allowed our athletes to compete and succeed against the world. We were too naïve to understand that Olympic athletes often serve as fodder for jostling governments. Think of the multiple boycotts by countries based on political stances, the scoring scandals concerning figure skating, and, more tragically, the 1972 terrorist attacks on the Israeli Olympic team. We young Americans were sure that the GDR, with its communist lack of competitive determination and nonmeritocracy, needed steroids to give it the unfair advantage that occasionally permitted it a victory. That American baseball now finds itself forever tainted by those same drug-enhanced performances we kids had sniggered over has justifiably eroded the public's fragile trust. And I can't help but think that the competitiveness that pushes players to use steroids—and then deny it—finds its genesis in the lower leagues.

In perhaps the culminating irony, it took these eastern German kids to remind me that it is possible to participate in a sport simply for pleasure. Players ran out to their positions and bounced in place as they waited for the next batter to step up. For each bad throw or poor swing, they laughed and good-naturedly cajoled one another. These kids demonstrated a thrill with playing ball that contrasts with the slump-shouldered, workmanlike attitude so many kids bring to the Little League fields. No one even kept track of the score.

The German teams played only for an inning after we arrived, then the game ended. As the kids separated out their gloves, bats, and hats, they shook hands, a German custom when arriving at or leaving any social occasion. That these players didn't have to line up and be forced to parade toward one another—the American hand-slapping as regimented as the games themselves—lent the scene an air of guilelessness that baseball in America seems perhaps incapable of recovering. It was the most satisfying inning of baseball I had seen in a long time.

And, Dizzy, there were no umpires. There was no need.

The trouble with all these shelves of stuff is: how can you ever really know what is fact, what fiction, and what still lies hidden?
—TIMOTHY GARTON ASH, discussing Stasi files in *The File*

9. The Class That Doesn't Exist in the Country That Once Did

As my creative writing class began one afternoon halfway into the university semester, Christoph raised his hand and said in his heavily accented English, "At home this weekend, I was talking with one of my former school teachers. When I told her that I was taking creative writing this semester, she said, 'This cannot be. Such a course does not exist.'"

I raised my eyebrows and lifted my palms, motioning outward in a slow arc that took in the brightly lit room, the furnishings, the dozen people. My gesture asked, "What is all this then?"

Everyone laughed.

"I'm not surprised," I admitted. "Whenever I am asked what I teach here, I save this course for last because I know it is going to raise questions. Like your teacher, some even try to convince me that I must be mistaken. Or they just shake their heads."

Contrary to Christoph's former teacher's contention, our class—with its lively, engaged students, interesting subject matter, and learning clearly taking place—existed each time the twelve of us gathered in that large-windowed and often sun-filled room. But her supposition makes sense. That creative writing is not well known in Germany becomes a little more understandable when one also knows that writing of any kind is not commonly taught in German universities. Students are expected to know how to write when they arrive at college. Indeed, writing as part of a class can be fairly uncommon. Several of my students who were majoring in both German and English told me they had done practically no writing in their years of German studies and only occasionally in English classes.

Teaching a class in a country where the concept of that course does not exist is like searching for a second side to the one-sided Möbius strip. Still, eleven curious students were brave enough to try, having read only the title "Creative Writing" in a course guide. Even that was a misnomer, though, as the only genre we studied was flash fiction. Also known as microfiction, short short story, sudden fiction, and several other terms, such writing is marked by its brevity and usually limited to a certain number of words, say 250 or 500. I chose flash fiction because I felt the genre's length would allow students to experience some immediate success. They would not spend weeks struggling over a twenty-page story only to find its premise untenable. Instead, as writers squinting into the intensity of language, they could create revealing glimpses into characters and lives.

My students immediately informed me that, like creative writing classes, flash fiction does not exist in Germany. The Möbius strip twists on itself. To introduce them to flash fiction as a genre, we began with the notion of genre itself. As second-language learners, my students understood that when learning a language, they acquire its grammatical conventions by comparing what they already know with what they are learning, thereby figuring out how the new language operates differently. I persuaded them that just as there are grammar rules a language user adheres to, so too are there genre conventions that a writer follows—and that these differ from genre to genre. As Janet Cary Eldred says in *Sentimental Attachments*, "Genre, like metaphors, define, which is to say that they open and close possibilities by delimiting." Adequately employing genre expectations and conventions—the grammar of a genre—means learning to use a language in all the depth available to that genre.

I also had to convince my students that genres differ from one another not only in form but also in the worldview available through the form. The grammar of the genre influences what we are able to say and how we perceive the world through that genre. So introducing German students to flash fiction required not only studying examples of the genre but also making students realize that the worldview offered by flash fiction was one they were unfamiliar with and had to learn to write within. To reinforce flash fiction's being an English-language phenomenon, we conducted the whole course in English—discussions, group work, readings, and writings.

As I looked at early drafts and spoke with students, I found that the most successful writers did not simply translate from German to English. They realized that to begin in German would require that they first translate the genre into German. By writing in English, they thought within the genre and within the worldview provided by the genre.

And yet I related more to the students who tried to write flash fiction in German and then translate it into English. I too struggle to understand the "genre" of Germany in general and the GDR in particular, and because I cannot master the language, I ally myself with these students. Still, ease with the language would not have been enough for me. Just as Christoph's former teacher was convinced that a course in creative writing couldn't exist despite what he told her, so too does my East Germany exist without existing. Only in words is it imagined and reimagined. My life and East Germany are the rails of a train track that come together only at the horizon point that can never be reached, no matter how much one moves toward it.

Let me be clear in what I am saying, though I place it here near the end of the book where it may remain hidden from those who skim book jackets, openings, and back cover blurbs: *In the Shadows of a Fallen Wall* is inherently unsuccessful. I have my experiences, I have my imagination, but I have no genre on which to draw, no sense of form that allows me to understand East Germany. My GDR is that other side of the Möbius strip, the unreachable one. Thus, I have had to create anew by drawing upon what I know. The rest of this piece offers an amalgamation of forms: narratives, anecdotes, jokes, photographs, and flash fiction that I wrote alongside my students that semester. These parts do not speak directly to one another but instead whisper across the page. Like stars in a constellation, they linger in each other's vicinity, their role in the larger shape determined by those who stand outside the constellation.

Just as genres provide worldviews, so too do societies. When a society collapses, a void does not replace the prior worldview; new perspectives are adopted or imposed to replace the old. As with genres, how we read the new worldview depends very much on how we understood the old ones. We always overlay the new onto the old, accumulating our truths.

When Manuela Linde was a young college graduate starting her career as a tour guide in the former East Germany, she lived in an apartment tucked under the rafters of a medieval structure that was in disrepair in part because there was little money to upgrade or tear down dwellings. Moreover, her particular building remained the property of a West German, so the city's communal dwellings administration saw no reason to invest money in a house that was not theirs. Rats had the run of the walls, sometimes also overtaking the floors and furniture. The roof leaked and she had to catch the water in buckets. The stairs were rotting. The bathroom was on a different floor and shared with several other inhabitants. Hot water was a rarity. One winter, the pipes froze and were never fixed, leaving her without running water. Manuela is a pragmatist. She doesn't romanticize living there. Instead, she is grateful that she met Wilfried, with whom she would often stay to get out of the apartment prior to their marriage.

One evening when we had the Lindes over for dinner, we began talking about the *Weihnachtsmarkt*. Manuela said that in former times the market wasn't very interesting, that there wasn't anything to buy: "There were more rides then, but those have now been replaced by all the shops with their many offerings."

The next day, we had coffee with the Gundermans, a retired couple in their early sixties and the parents of the woman we sublet from. When I asked Frau Gunderman what the *Weihnachtsmarkt* was like during former times, she went into a long discussion about how much nicer it was then. She described how the fairy tale area was so much bigger and in better shape than it is now. "And the items for sale are too expensive for people to afford," she lamented. "Plus, all the shops sell the same thing."

Such conversations reflect a generational difference, one that is fairly representative of the post-GDR era. In *Reflections on the Human Condition*, Eric Hoffer argues, "In a time of drastic changes it is the learners who inherit the future. The learned usually find themselves equipped in a world that no longer exists." The Lindes are the learners of Hoffer's declaration; the Gundermans the learned. The Gundermans see their lives through the GDR lens. They were forced into retirement by the reunification of East and West. The Lindes, however, have benefited from the fall of the Wall, with Manuela securing a very good job as the international officer at the University of Erfurt and Wilfried managing to find steady employment, even if he's overqualified for it. They own their house in the woods and two cars. They frequently vacation outside of Germany. The transition marked by the *Wende* has provided each family a new perspective on life, but how propitious that view depends on one's view of future potentialities.

So I was surprised that some of my students demonstrated attitudes of the "learned." Those in a course on essay writing I offered for future elementary school teachers were between age nine and eleven when the Wall came down. Though I imagined they were young enough that the GDR system would not have been completely ingrained in their thinking, many carried with them at least a partial GDR perspective as they negotiated their role within the new system.

Socialist East German education differed from West German education in its emphasis on camaraderie, science and technology, and links to the adult working life. As John Ardagh says in *Germany and the Germans*, "The philosophy was that all young people, however intellectual, should acquire some basic technical skill." This makes sense in a system where the worker is revered. Everyone, no matter what he attains, was to identify with the worker, on whom the system purportedly rests. However, this turned out not to be the case, as the system itself, rather than the worker, drove the system. The worker had little to no say about his or her contribution. One would imagine students understood, at least implicitly, that the educational aims and training were entwined with and complicit in the regime's downfall.

For one in-class essay, I asked the students to respond to a relatively straightforward question: As future teachers, what would you change about the current education system? There is little chance that such a question about altering the system—and the students' ideas for doing so—would have been posed during GDR times. Then, university life was quite regimented, boring even. Students couldn't pick which courses they were going to take and often couldn't choose the subject they wanted to major in. But once one graduated, a job was assured. Now there are not enough jobs. A government-mandated increase in the low student-to-teacher ratio of GDR times in combination with a declining population has meant fewer opportunities for teacher employment. This means most of my students would have to move to the west to find work. Not only will they be living in the still somewhat foreign western part of the country, they are going to be teachers in a system that they did not grow up in. And they will take their beliefs founded in an East German system with them.

A majority of students suggested in their responses to my question—without saying so directly—that returning, at least in part, to East German–style education would improve the system. One insisted, "The eight a.m. class starting time in schools is too late." She argued that 7:15—when most GDR school days began—is "a more appropriate time to begin lessons." She is not alone in this feeling. Everything still runs earlier in eastern Germany. Many people arrive at work by 7:00 a.m. and leave prior to 4:00 p.m. Streetcar schedules accommodate this, running most frequently from 6:00 to 8:00 a.m. and 2:00 to 4:00 p.m.

This same student went on to claim that there was a "fissure between the school time and leisure time." Since the German school day often ends by 1:00 p.m., she offered that "afternoons with classmates and teachers could improve the relationship between teachers and pupils." Such an idea again suggests a return to GDR times, when authority figures structured free time for young students via field trips, crafts, or even recycling projects. The motivation for the recycling differed from the current rationale for doing so. Rather than collecting bottles, cans, or paper for ecological reasons, GDR students did so because of the scarcity of natural resources. They would turn these objects in at recycling centers to meet the demand. With such a need, unstructured time equaled wasted time. And doing so kept the young under the watchful eyes of authorities and out of the trouble that free time fosters.

When the GDR disappeared, my essay-writing students were young enough that they were largely immune from being personally affected by the system's problems. Indeed, most anyone who grew up in the GDR whom I have spoken with discusses the early years of school as a wonderful time for kids. Yet this particular group of students really is a transition generation. Having been educated in both systems, they espouse old and new ideals. This can be seen in one student's discussion of school facilities. First, she complained about the furniture: "Students write on and carve their names and such into the tables, and place gum underneath them." She then reminisced about how things were in her early days as a student. Clearly, she wanted to return to those days under the GDR when students showed respect—no matter the means to get them to do so—for classroom furnishings. But her second complaint showed a desire to embrace Western technologies. She noted that schools lack computers, video machines, televisions, even cassette players. While wishing to return to the attitudes demonstrated toward school property during GDR times, she also wanted the benefit of drawing upon the latest western technological advances. She reminded me of the woman in Timothy Garton Ash's *The File* who believes that the fall of the Wall allowed her children to have the best of both worlds—a childhood in the socialist GDR and an adulthood in the capitalist, reunified Germany.

Not surprisingly, the East German rite of passage to adulthood has itself gone through a transition. GDR teenagers participated in *Jugendweihe*. This "youth dedication ceremony" offers a secular form of confirmation that was adopted by the East German state to both replace confirmation and initiate youth into adult socialist society. Since the Wall's fall, youngsters still take part in *Jugendweihe*, but the ceremony now serves as eighth-grade graduation.

Celebrants receive a book that, during GDR times, was called *Space, Earth, Man*, but is now called *Between No Longer and Not Yet*. Of course, the latter speaks to the students' position between youth and adulthood, but the shift in titles also reflects how, for eastern Germans, the world that was once represented in terms of solidity and scientific assuredness—and East Germans' rightful place within this universe—has changed into one of ambiguity, dissonance, and adaptation. This new historical perspective tells people that they can *no longer* rely on the safety and security provided by the communist state, even if it was founded on misnomers and distrust. More importantly, what has replaced it is *not yet* fully realized. Someday, life in eastern Germany—the title implies—will be a new genre through which people can read themselves. At the moment, the genre conventions are not fully articulated; people do not know how to read their future, let alone their present. And there is no scapegoat to blame for these uncertainties, as existed in the past.

Abell stood on the gallows: gaunt, prepared, and smirking. Some might say leering. The rope itched against his swollen neck. The sun sank low behind the swaying crowd. Though no shadows reached Abell, he shivered.

"At what do you grin?" came a call from the crowd.

"You," Abell taunted.

"Why?"

"You know the answer," slobbered Abell, spit dribbling into his beard.

There was no response, just an audible murmuring.

"Does your fear keep you from speaking?" Abell asked.

Again, no response.

"How long must I suffer you?"

The reply came from the hangman, whose quick motion startled those in the front rows.

Abell, whom the crowd once believed to have represented their hopes for the future but whom they now suspected was responsible for the scourge of the present, fell through the trap door.

His bare feet scuffed faint arcs in the dirt.

Those not in the first row stood high on their toes to glimpse the spectacle.

Long shadows reached toward Abell's slowly rotating body as the crowd filed past. New spittle, cast by former friends and neighbors, trickled down Abell's face, crossed his lips and dropped into the tangle of hair on his chin.

The hangman stood nearby, wearing Abell's shoes. No one said a word, not even the hangman, who found that they pinched his toes.

The rats would begin their feasting with the onset of darkness.

Knowing our year abroad would take us to Regensburg for those six weeks of intensive German lessons then onto Berlin for the orientation session and finally to Erfurt, we packed two large boxes of household goods, winter clothes, and various other items the four of us would not need until we settled into our *Plattenbau* lifestyle. We shipped these by sea—the slow route—hoping they would arrive in Erfurt about the same time we did. Two boxes for the whole year. Everything else would be borrowed, bought, or brought in the suitcases we carried with us.

As January drew to an end—almost halfway through our year—one box still had not arrived. At least it had not made it to our apartment. We would eventually learn that the box had, at one point, visited in Germany. Back in October the boxes had arrived at the port of Hamburg as a pair. But for reasons we would not figure out until much later, one was returned to the United States. Because the U.S. postal workers in our small-town post office recalled my being there a few months earlier and explaining how this was all we had to live on for a year, they promptly shipped the package back, ignoring the German authorities' notation since it was in a language they did not understand. When the box again arrived in Hamburg, it was returned a second time. The U.S. post office sent it right back; the Hamburg authorities returned it. We will never know how many times this transatlantic ping-pong match repeated itself.

Unaware of any of this, we investigated the box's non-arrival through several different agencies. No one could seem to find the box, only where it had been, like a fish that jumps unseen, the rippling water the only evidence of it having been there. Finally, we wrote off the package, hoping that we might catch up to it upon returning to the United States. We borrowed winter jackets and gloves that were in the

Euro colors of the day: purples, reds, and golds. We also resigned ourselves to Tara's not being able to play in the school band, as we had shipped her clarinet along with the coats. She had borrowed a clarinet only to discover that those in Germany are constructed differently from American ones, and she was unable to adjust to the new fingering.

One day in late January, the English department's secretary ran into my office waving a letter above her head. A package with my name had arrived at the Erfurt customs office. I borrowed a friend who owned a car, and we rushed out to the *Zollamt*. The package heaved onto the counter was still taped shut but appeared to have been dropped from the top of the Fernsehturm. The official demanded I open the box in front of him. The customs declaration slip had gone missing, so he wanted to see the contents. This was why the box had never appeared. Without the customs slip, entry into Germany was repeatedly refused. However, the package had finally been forwarded because the return address label had also been ripped off in the last trip across the Atlantic. The German authorities had no place to send the package back to. Instead of destroying it, they decided in their magnanimity to finally forward it to the *Zollamt* nearest our address.

It had been so long since we had sent the box to ourselves that it was like Christmas all over again as the four of us sat on the living room floor and pulled out items we had forgotten we sent. Roberta happily replaced dull kitchen knives with her favorite 6-inch chef's knife, which the customs official somehow allowed me to take after my awkward explanation of how important it was to my wife, an accomplished cook. Tara hugged her clarinet to her chest, then eventually joined the city's band and played in over two dozen *Jugendweihe* ceremonies, so many that she could recite the ceremony word for German word. More important, she was so beloved by the band that at the last performance she was presented with a huge bouquet of flowers, bringing her to tears. Yet, the largest items—our winter jackets—we left in the box. We continued to wear our borrowed coats. They were no warmer, no more comfortable. But with their European styling and bold colors, they made us feel less foreign and more a part of the cityscape as we moved through the Erfurt we imagined our lives to be.

AMERICAN, THE BEAUTIFUL

After disembarking the ship, they were directed up a long flight of open stairs.

Dragging his luggage on either side, Heinrich was breathing heavily when he reached the top. A man pointed at Heinrich. A woman took him by the arm.

"What is your name?" she asked, leading him toward the doctor.

Heinrich did not reply.

"Sprechen Sie Deutsch?" she offered.

"Ja," he answered.

"Wie heissen Sie?"

Heinrich, who had decided to change his name as soon as he got to America, replied "Henry."

"Welcome, stranger," she said.

Henry did not understand. "Willkommen streng"? Why was she welcoming him severely to America?

Speaking slowly and clearly in his native tongue, for he could tell her German was not good, Henry asked, "Warum darf ich nicht mit den anderen aus meinem Boot sein?"—"Why am I not allowed to be with the others from my boat?"

Her knowledge of German exhausted, the woman did not

respond. Henry turned and she smiled at him. He thought he would not see another American so beautiful.

The doctor conducted a quick examination, then used a piece of chalk to place an H on the lapel of Henry's shirt. Henry smiled. He thought the H stood for "Henry." It stood for "heart."

Few were aboard ship as it steamed back toward Hamburg. No longer able to discern land off the stern, a man splashed unnoticed into the chilly Atlantic. A few concentric rings quickly disappeared while he thought of his American love and her harsh welcome for a man named Heinrich.

Q: How do you double the worth of a Trabi?
A: Fill the gas tank.

When Wilfried first told me this, I laughed, as did he. But when I thought about it later, this joke, like so much comedy, is funny precisely because of the cultural assumptions implicit in the context. The humor results from the status that the Trabi, the diminutive of Trabant, once held in East Germany. These small, low-horsepower, high-polluting automobiles with Duroplast bodies (a cardboard-like plastic created using either cotton or sheep's wool) symbolize the communist state as much as the Big Three automakers epitomize Detroit.

Wilfried informed me that when the Wall came down *Car and Driver*, or some such magazine, got hold of a Trabi and put it through the same paces as other test cars. When it came to measuring the time of acceleration from 0 to 60 miles per hour, the researchers gave up after three minutes because the Trabi had yet to reach 60. During GDR times, the speed limit on highways was 100 kilometers per hour, which works

out to about 64 miles per hour, a speed that apparently can be reached only when a Trabi is headed downhill.

While the Trabi represents the most observable remnant of failed socialist values—or perhaps because of this—it has also attained icon status in post-GDR Germany. Trabants are collected and revered by enthusiasts, who have formed Trabi clubs to share their knowledge about and passion for the little car that barely could. Trabis in German parades are as de rigueur as Shriners are at American parades. These are not just intact versions of the classic Trabant, many of which can still be seen driving around east German streets. Rather, the parade-goers are customized—souped-up versions, convertibles, and stretch limos among them. Many businesses use Trabis as mobile advertisements in the parades. While we were in Germany, a contest was underway to find the most beautiful Trabi. If the popularity of these little cars seems paradoxical now, a different irony surrounded Trabis during GDR times. Then, used Trabis often sold for more than new ones since the wait from the time one placed an order—no showroom, no options to choose from—was up to fifteen years. For more money, one could avoid the wait and purchase a used Trabant immediately.

The Trabant even has literary status in a genre that has had to reinvent itself since the fall of the Wall. In his spy thriller *Dead Ground*, Gerald Seymour makes the Trabant the critical plot element. Tracy Barnes, a young British woman acting as a go-between, sees her East German lover, who is spying for the West, killed during a botched reconnaissance attempt on the East German Baltic coast. She is forced to flee the scene because she must cross the Berlin checkpoint before midnight or her cover will be blown. Near the end of the book, protagonist Josh Mantle realizes Barnes's drive from Rerik to Berlin could not have occurred under these time constraints if, as Barnes alleges, she had driven a Trabant. The cars simply could not go fast enough to make the trip within the time period that she claimed. Mantle surmises that Barnes has double-crossed him and has served, in actuality, as a spy for the GDR. In a self-sacrificing heroic act, he turns in the woman he has fallen for and with whom he could have had the family he has always wanted, exchanging his personal happiness for moral certitude—all because of the speed-challenged Trabant.

Perhaps the Trabant failed so miserably because it was not even intended to be an automobile. The original design, that of a three-wheeled motorcycle, was altered late in the process when a fourth wheel was added. The Trabi was often referred to as a "personal carrier" or "transporter," a cross between a motorcycle and a car. This attempt to create something out of two types of vehicle was similar to my creative writing students who attempted to write their flash fiction in German first. The inability to think within a nonexistent genre did not allow them to create an accomplished product. Similarly, my understanding of East Germany is always a genre of my own creation, founded on stories from those who were there and artifacts removed from their context.

Toward the end of the semester, I expressed to my students an interest in wanting to ride in a Trabant. One notices their prevalence because of the loud whine from the two-stroke engine and the smoke from the poor exhaust system as they accelerate up the street. I followed their trail of pollution each time one passed by. Unfortunately, no one in the class owned one.

A few days after the semester ended, one of the students e-mailed to tell me her friend owned a Trabi and had offered to take me for a ride. Here was my chance to actually ride in and maybe drive one. I would certainly take a photo and put it next to the one of me standing by the Mercedes we had rented for a trip around Germany. However, the e-mail went on, the friend lived in Berlin and would have to drive down to Erfurt, a multihour trip even in a reliable automobile. I thought of *The Dead Zone*, the long drive ending in some futile escape attempt. I declined the kind invitation, knowing not even the Trabi could take me to that horizon point where the genres of past and present meet.

THE NEW ECONOMY

Every few months a young woman knocks on my apartment door. She holds before her a bag filled with bars of white soap. These are neither trick nor treat. They come from a very wealthy man. Because he has so much money, he can do things the rest of us cannot, like give away his soap after the name—with its curves and wavy lines—has worn off.

I take the bag by the handles and thank her. We talk nervously about nothing. Her skin is smooth, and I like the way she dips her head as she tosses her hair. I want to invite her in, but I cannot come up with an excuse for doing so. She is thirty years my junior; I do not own a shirt as crisp as hers. We say our good-byes, then I shut the door without turning away.

One evening after she appeared, I lowered myself into the lukewarm water of the tub and reached for the bag. Instead of removing one bar, I held the bag before me and tipped it. The bars splashed, sank for a moment, then rose to the surface again. There they floated, dozens of white bars of blankness. Cells from the very wealthy man began to slough off, forming a film on the water's surface. My penis drifted languidly in the depths below.

A friend advised us to spend our year abroad traveling Europe, seeing as much as we could. He urged us to take out loans, if necessary, to pay for the trips. This man, who is from my parents' generation, has traveled around the world, lived in different places in the United States, and led a somewhat alternative and enviable lifestyle as a painter, rodeo cowboy, and gentleman farmer. Yet even as he implored this constant travel on us, I knew we wouldn't follow his advice. Roberta and I had decided that we did not want breadth of coverage during our year; we wanted depth of experience.

We did not want to be constant tourists, hopping from town to town. Tim Bell, our American friend but decades-long German resident, once declared, "The problem with being in Europe is that there's too much culture and not enough life." We wanted to experience the life of the culture, not simply the culture without life.

We wanted to stand outside in the cold next to the bratwurst huts, smoke from the grill pouring across us, and eat

the local favorite, Thuringian-style brats, a foot-long, finely minced pork and beef sausage with a small clutch of bread around the middle that serves more to protect one's fingers than as part of the meal.

We wanted on a Friday evening to carry home our case of beer—a plastic reusable crate filled with returnable bottles that we toted between us—and have the man passing in the other direction wave, wink, and say knowingly, "Have a good weekend!"

We wanted the opportunity to walk to the little *Weinstube* tucked on the edge of a park, where we would sit outside and not order the tasteless food except for the meat and cheese tray, and where we somehow found it gratifying to be ignored by our favorite waitress.

We wanted to return again to the Italian restaurant along the banks of the river in town where, because of our raucous and free-spending meal there with friends visiting from the United States, on our next visit we were greeted heartily and promptly offered complimentary glasses of *Sekt*, German-style champagne.

We wanted to have Tara attend a German school and have her enjoy the experience so much that on the day we were locking up the apartment for the last time, she asked, "When can I come back?"

We wanted to walk Callan to the neighborhood kindergarten where, at the top of the buildings steps, we would find a carriage complete with a sleeping baby, the mother inside dropping off the older sibling and not fearing that anything might happen to her newborn. And we ourselves would leave Callan with total strangers who spoke no English but whom we were confident loved and cared for her as if she had been and would be attending school there forever.

In these nontourist encounters we succeeded. And, yet, all this is not enough. My contemplation of this land must forever remain one step removed from the original, my words existing among that which I experienced, that which lies hidden, and that which cannot be.

10. Whatever You Do, Don't Look Down

The Kölner Spielecircus, small by circus standards—two men, a woman, and some props—stood upon a large, red semicircular tarp spread out before us. One man introduced himself as Pelle, which I have since learned is a nickname that comes from the Anglo-Norman and means a tall, thin man. Close to six and a half feet tall, Pelle wore a blue shirt, red vest, yellow bow tie, and checkered pants. His gray hair made him appear a little old for this line of work.

Pelle scanned the crowd as he spoke into the microphone. I thought his glance stopped momentarily on me. Was I about to be selected to participate? Was this circus not just *spielen* but *mitspielen*, not just playing but playing with? The man's eyes kept moving, but more quickly. I knew he was only confirming me as his choice.

I didn't want to stand before this audience.

The Damms had invited us to attend the event. Thomas had done contract work for a local union. Having joined with another union, they were putting on a celebratory dinner. Thomas received an invitation, noting the circus performance, and asked if we would like to bring the kids and come along. "Sure," I agreed, thinking I would be entertained, not part of the entertainment.

The day had begun badly enough. A burning throat, stomach ache, and bouts of dizziness kept me on the couch. But I finally decided to go, hoping that the several-kilometer walk through the woods to the Waldhaus would have me feeling better. Besides, I didn't want to miss the chance to share in the kids' delight as much as I wanted to see the performance for myself.

That early March day was muddy from melting snow. The hike—with four adults and four girls—was slow going as we slalomed around the sloppiest parts of the trail. Still, I found myself growing stronger in the fresh air. Arriving at the Waldhaus later than we expected, we entered a large room with a high, vaulted, wooden ceiling and walls covered in crests. But it was the people who caught my attention.

While a few wore jeans, as did we, most wore varying degrees of dress clothes, up to and including formal wear. No one had muddy shoes and pant cuffs like ourselves; I was sure they had not trekked through the woods to get here. There were also no other children. Either this crowd of more than a hundred was childless or they interpreted the invitation differently than Thomas. Most everyone was already seated, and the only place left that would fit eight was right before the large tarp. As if the performers had been awaiting our arrival, the circus began soon after we sat down.

Pelle stopped studying the audience. He swiveled and pointed his index finger directly at me, and I felt dizzy all over again. I turned around and held open my hands, imploring those at our table to help. They laughed and urged me forward. I reluctantly stood up.

Being picked out of the crowd was like being awarded a Fulbright. You know there is a group of people from which one or more will be chosen. You know you are being sized up, compared, studied. But you are never exactly sure of the criteria on which you are being judged. *Why me?* I had asked after receiving the award. Immediately, I felt as if I didn't belong, that I didn't deserve it, that I was some sort of imposter.

And now I had again been chosen for reasons I could only conjecture: near the front, casually dressed, of slight build, and apparently with some look of willingness that belied my feelings. Since no one in the crowd knew me, they must have thought me a plant, a part of the performance. Yet I was about to be paraded in front of a group of possibly censorious strangers and asked to perform a trick that was absolutely unknown to me—and which I was sure to fail at. I would soon be found out.

But I might just as well ask the question—of both the circus and Fulbright—in a different way: *What had I done to deserve this?* The first few months of our Fulbright had been filled with a muddiness that seemed to splatter across us. In addition to the expected problems—moving into the *Plattenbau* apartment a third the size of our house, Roberta trying to finish her dissertation from a continent away, getting two kids established in school, and dealing with the culture and language problems we all faced—so many other incidents added to our feeling that we were trudging, not skipping, through the year.

At the university, I had been misinformed about the content of my courses and had to completely recreate two of them a few days before classes began. Nor was my first office within my department. Instead, I was dispatched to a small room at the end of a corridor of administrative offices in a different building. The day I was finally given an office near my colleagues three months after the semester began, a party broke out in the hallway, and I saw what I had been missing. As for the computer woes that accompanied all this, I'll just say that East and West Germans talked to each other more easily before the Wall fell than my Mac would communicate with the PC-based university computer system. When I wanted to print a one-page document, the labyrinthine procedure took upward of fifteen minutes.

The Escort being stolen and driven into the ditch was followed by a month-long introduction to the intricacies of German bureaucracy that included the overworked police department, two disinterested repair garages, an uncooperative insurance company, and the ultimate loss of our primary mode of weekend transportation.

And our box of belongings ended up in that game of continental hot potato, reaching us only after five or seven trips across the Atlantic. We will never know for sure.

But this was the comedy; these were stories we had already begun to laugh about. There was also sorrow. Roberta's grandmother in Augsburg, the one she had not seen in twenty-five years and who had yet to meet her great-grandchildren, died shortly after we arrived in Germany. So, too, did our neighbor across the street from us in New Jersey. The wife of an old friend, Wilfried Linde's mother, my best friend's mother . . . all passed away.

This was not the way it was supposed to turn out. My previous German teaching experience had been very difficult. My unfamiliarity with the language, the isolated living situation, a heavy workload on top of several failed attempts to get a dissertation up and running, the failed relationship that refused to end, and most of all my father's death had cast a pall over that period. This stay in Germany was supposed to erase those memories; instead, it often seemed to pick up where those had left off.

Pelle asked me my name, which, when I said the very un-German Sanford into the microphone, he asked me to say again. He repeated my name for the crowd, said something quickly, then turned away from me to prepare himself. I was sure he had said, "Zieh bitte die Schuhe aus"—take your shoes off, please—but I doubted myself. There was no way I was going to stand shoeless before these strangers without being sure that is what Pelle had commanded. I wasn't ready to be the comedy too.

In the meantime, Pelle handed the microphone to the woman, who interpreted my lack of movement as non-understanding and asked whether it was better if she spoke in English. Sure, I nodded before thinking. So she announced to everyone that in addition to enjoying the show, they would get to practice their English. Even that statement was probably not understood by most in the crowd of middle-aged East Germans whose required second language in school would have been Russian. If it wasn't clear before that I didn't belong, it was now.

Once I had removed my shoes, Pelle stood me in front of him, facing the audience, while he squatted behind me. He had me place my feet on his thighs, then he grabbed onto them and had me stand up, arms upraised. An easy trick, I was thinking to myself when, without warning, Pelle dipped his head between my legs and I was sitting on his shoulders. Then, he commanded: right foot on right shoulder, hold both hands, left foot on left shoulder, and up you go. Up I went, my head some twelve feet above the floor. While I had felt better after the walk, once my head joined the heat and cigarette smoke collecting near the ceiling, I was convinced I would lurch to one side or the other, ungraciously tumbling to the floor before the, no doubt, laughing crowd.

Yet when I stood on Pelle's shoulders, not only did I not feel bad, I had a sudden burst of confidence, perhaps one might even say an epiphany—if only of a minor nature. I could use all the clichés to describe this: it was the pinnacle, summit, zenith, *Höhepunkt*—high point—of this yearlong German experience. But these would be exaggerations. Indeed, to try to say that this represents my Fulbright experience would be an oversimplification. A year cannot be defined by a photographed moment.

Still, it was an instant of clarity in the Fulbright year. Our lives had, after all the initial turmoil, begun to settle into a routine defined by its lack of lows or dizzying highs. The Fulbright, I came to see, is not a year *out of* your life, but a year *in* your life. The world goes on. Thieves still steal cars, things don't go according to plan, people die.

And, I realized that despite the feelings of isolation and alienation one often feels during the long year that passes so quickly, I had done none of this alone. Below me, I could see Fulbright, the one in the red vest who has provided me this view. I saw Germany and Germans, the country and people that had welcomed me with open arms—even if some were used for jimmying locks. I looked to my friends the Damms, who, like the Lindes and others, had invited us into their lives. I also saw my family, for one person may receive a Fulbright but the whole family lives it. And I saw me, not an imposter, below me—flawed, sometimes frustrated, ultimately grateful.

I held out my arms like a gymnast after nailing the landing, and the crowd of strangers smiled and clapped. I looked to my table of family and friends, who laughed and applauded louder. I looked to the ground. Oh wait, you are not supposed to do that. But here too I see a parallel with the Fulbright experience, which seems to be all about not looking down, for Fulbright causes you to lose your grounding, your foundations, your sense of security. With the recipients' consent, Fulbright puts them on a pedestal then kicks it out from under them. Everyone hopes there is no loud crash or broken bones.

But what our stay abroad ultimately had done was to reconfirm something I already believed: how we interpret our experiences is as important as the experiences themselves. During our stay in Erfurt, a colleague from the United States, Ned Eckhardt, who was visiting western Germany, drove over to see us. Ned is interested in Meister Eckhart, a thirteenth- and fourteenth-century mystic with whom he almost shares a name. The earlier Eckhart is believed to have been born in or near Erfurt, moved through the hierarchies of the Catholic church, and died in 1327 while being tried for heresy. Because of Eckhart's ties to Erfurt, Ned wanted to tour the town.

The day, like so many in Erfurt, was cold, and light rain fell throughout our tour. We stopped at the Predigerkirche, or Preacher's Church, where Meister Eckhart had been the prior. It was not open because they could not afford to heat it. We were able to find Meister-Eckhart-Strasse and Meister-Eckhart-Brücke. Ned stood near the bridge while we took pictures in the rain. Eventually we made our way to an Irish pub, where we spent the rest of the afternoon drinking beer while Ned regaled us with stories from the homeland. Ned also reminded us about that which we had grown used to. He was filled with awe and admiration not only for the beauty and history of Erfurt, but also for our lifestyle in this former East German city and how well our kids were doing. By six the next morning, Ned was gone. "Going over the Wall today," he said as he waved and drove away, leaving me standing in the still-damp street. After returning to the States, he sent a note of thanks in which he said, "Our paths crossed in the Old Country, and it was one of the times of my life."

As I stood on those red-vested shoulders, I looked back up and smiled at the crowd. Suddenly, I heard "Komm runter!"—Get down!—hissed at me. However, only when our plane lifted off the runway in Frankfurt and ascended did I finally do so. For despite all the difficulties and all the setbacks, too soon my family and I knew we would be back in the United States, reminiscing about the time of our lives.

The past is a foreign country:
they do things differently there.
—L. P. HARTLEY

11. In Former Times

I wrote the last line of "Whatever You Do, Don't Look
Down"—the one suggesting we would soon be reminiscing
about the time of our lives—while still living in Germany.
Reminiscing has, of course, a positive connotation. If we are
reminiscing, we are nostalgic for a time gone by, one that we
enjoy replaying in our thoughts or through words. We are
musing about, not dwelling upon, that past. My implication
in writing that line was that whatever had happened during
our year abroad, once we returned home to our small New
Jersey town, we would look back on that period with fond-
ness as chronological and spatial distance intervened. But
I also had, in writing that line while we lived in Erfurt, already transformed the present into a memory.

Our memories are not vessels into which we pour our experiences. They are ongoing. Even as we live our lives, we
are already placing those experiences into the narrative
through which we tell our own story. In pointing out the influence of memory in *The File*, Timothy Garton Ash says,
"What we usually call 'my life' is a constantly rewritten version of our own past. 'My life' is the mental autobiography
with which and by which we all live." The *experience* is immediately translated into the *experienced*. Our lives are little

more than memories revisited, relived, reclaimed, revised, re-presented. And the memories themselves are altered by new experiences. Garton Ash confirms this, referring to "memories that change slowly, always, with every passing second, but now and then dramatically, after some jolt or revelation." For Garton Ash, discovering that a Stasi file had been kept on him and that people he trusted had informed on him caused such a "dividing line."

For East Germans, the "jolt" occurred with the fall of the Wall and the changes that accompanied it. When I shared an earlier version of this book with Manuela, she commented on my frequent use of "in former times," a phrase she had said often and I had assumed was common parlance. "I did not think anything special when saying that, but perhaps it describes what is our two lives: one in the GDR and one in the FRG," she said. And Manuela demonstrated the role of memory in such disruptions: "The way from one to the other went smoothly although quickly, but now . . . it feels like a cut. The life before and the life after."

Unlike East Germans, we knew what our futures held upon our return to the United States. I believed our shift to former times would be a moderate transition, one filled with reminiscing. I was correct, but only momentarily. Just as Garton Ash had to reassess and revise his memories after discovering and reading his Stasi file, so too would our pasts require reconsideration.

Because the German university calendar extends into mid-July, we did not return to the United States until August 2, 2001, five days shy of a year after we last left America. That afternoon, we walked through customs at Philadelphia International Airport, leaving behind our German lives. We returned to the United States with most of the meager belongings we had hauled over, again shipping items we could do without for a while. Not all were the same as those we shipped over. Roberta did not want to wait again on her cutlery, so we tucked the eight-inch chef's knife into one of our checked bags. And Tara made sure she had her clarinet so she would be ready for marching band camp, which had already begun. Callan carried her most prized acquisition, Bubba, a flashlight-toting stuffed bear given to her by Clara from her personal collection. Bubba says phrases such as "Ich bin müde!" (I am tired), "Hey Kumpel, wollen wir Schafe zählen?" (Hey buddy, want to count sheep?), "Hey, spielst du mit meiner Taschenlampe?" (Hey, are you playing with my flashlight?), and "Hast du Angst?" (Are you anxious?). He even asks you to put him on his belly, but once you do so he proclaims that was not such a good idea after all. Most important, we brought back the stories in our heads, tales we hoped to tell. We were ready to reminisce about the time of our lives. But first we had to settle back into a life we once knew, a life that despite the reappearance of our house, car, and jobs right where we had left them, was now changed because we had changed.

In former times—that year in Germany—Roberta and I fretted over language situations we weren't prepared for. Yes, Bubba, we did have angst. While Tara and Callan may have also started out that way, neither ended the year still dreading every encounter, every knock on the door, every ring of the phone. Perhaps this was because we demanded they acquire the language in ways we did not require of ourselves.

The kids began attending their German schools in October, a few days after we moved to Erfurt. For Tara, the language deficiency was a hindrance at first, but she loved the attention she received for being an exotic American who brought in U.S. money for the other students to handle and who helped them practice their English. Perhaps most beneficial to the adjustment: not all of Tara's classes were overly difficult for her. She was, not surprisingly, the top student in English, though she learned some grammar concepts she hadn't been exposed to in the United States, as well as a good deal about British English, since this remains the commonly taught version in Europe. Early on, Tara corrected the teacher for referring to "maths" and was then herself corrected for not knowing this was the British term. Math itself, with its symbolic language, provided some equal footing. Plus, the German students were just starting to learn French that year. Tara—with what we have come to find out is her aptitude for languages—was among the top French students.

Similarly, we placed Callan in our neighborhood's kindergarten. The first day Roberta and she visited briefly so Callan could get a sense of where she would spend her days. She didn't want to leave, finally having the chance to be around other kids her same age after so many weeks in Regensburg.

The next morning, Roberta and I both went, hoping to buoy each other linguistically and emotionally. Callan had rarely been out of our sight the past two months. And although she had attended day care for two years back in the States, this time we were leaving her with a group of youngsters and adults who knew, at best, a few words of English. Most spoke none. As we walked among the neighborhood streets of tightly parked cars, we reminded Callan how much fun she could have when she was in kindergarten for the whole day.

Once inside, we stood among the mass of swirling students, Maypoles in a kindergarten dance. Callan clung to our legs. As Roberta and I tried to determine the best way to separate ourselves from her, the head teacher, Frau Lange, lowered herself to Callan's level, hugged her with both arms, and whispered "Mein Schatz, mein Schatz," a term of endearment meaning literally "my treasure" that she would use the whole year with Callan. Still holding tightly, Frau Lange removed one hand from Callan's back and waved us away. She understood how hard this was going to be both for Callan and for us. We did not linger nor did Callan see us slipping away. Frau Lange won us over with her astute judgment and loving manner.

Those first weeks and months spent adjusting were not without frustration for either of our girls. Tara once came home complaining about her history teacher lecturing on and on about "der Pabst." "Who the heck is this Pabst?" she exclaimed. While in America this is the name of a cheap beer, in Germany it is the word for "pope." A simple word, a lost lecture. Callan spent the first several weeks of kindergarten refusing to speak any German and continually blathering on to Frau Lange and others in a language they didn't understand. And whenever we parents tried to practice speaking German with her, Callan would bark, "Speak New Jersey!"

Yet by midwinter, Tara's and Callan's German abilities had increased to the point where they were both fairly fluent. Manuela told us that Callan bore no accent and Tara only the slightest. Even at home, our two girls would often play together for hours on end, never speaking a word of English. Tara informed us at one point that she no longer translated from English, thinking instead in German. On several occasions, when we asked her the meaning of something she had said, she couldn't tell us—not because she didn't know what she was saying, but because she simply didn't know how to say it in English. Callan conducted her at-play external monologue—that commentary so common to kids that age—in German. She sometimes confused the two languages, on more than one occasion asking of a TV show, "Are they speaking in English?" And both girls would often insert German into English sentences, such as "I ate the *ganzes* (entire) thing." Shortly before leaving, Callan proclaimed, "I am going to *vermisst* (miss) my friends."

One night late in January, Roberta received a phone call from a German friend of a friend we were making plans to visit and held a fifteen-minute conversation with her. Sitting on the couch chatting with Tara but also listening to Roberta, I was quite proud of her ability to keep up her end in German. After Roberta hung up, I was about to congratulate her when Tara burst out, "You two! You both sound so American. It's embarrassing."

And while I am sure Roberta dreaded that phone conversation, it became clear Tara and Callan eventually found encounters with Germans no more challenging than those with English speakers. Callan and a grocery store clerk once amused themselves with some sort of game they made up. The clerk would start and stop the vinyl belts used to move our purchases as Callan shifted items from one to the other. They bantered back and forth, Callan squealing in delight. Roberta and I stood at the end of one belt and quietly packed the groceries Callan allowed to proceed to us, unable to follow the lilting conversation even though the game was clearly one of repetition.

Roberta and I, on the other hand, never lost the constant dread of a conversation we couldn't control. We fretted over language situations we weren't prepared for, dreading every encounter, every knock on the door, every ring of the phone. This was perhaps our greatest burden: having to constantly expend energy considering how to communication with others—not just outside but even when at home in the apartment. Roberta explained it best in an article she wrote for *The Funnel*, the magazine of the German-American Fulbright Commission:

> Some days you ride high. You exchange spontaneous small talk with a stranger. You read entire newspaper articles without having to look up any words. You correctly formulate a sentence using the passive.
>
> Some days you are brought low. A child at the kindergarten tells you something with such stunning grammatical and semantic complexity that you can do nothing but nod and smile . . . A neighbor comes to the door one afternoon with a question. You ask him to please repeat it all more slowly because you are not quite sure you understood completely. *Langsamer*, he sighs. He tries again. You piece it together, sort of, but you feel that your graceless response is little help.

That "sort of" perfectly describes so many encounters. I "sort of" get what someone says. I "sort of" know how to respond. But, in conversation, "sort of" isn't good enough. For Roberta and me, if not the kids, returning to the United States allowed us the opportunity to finally exhale after a year of holding our breath in anticipation of words that constantly sought to betray us.

A few weeks after we returned, Callan began kindergarten. She excelled from the beginning, doing very well in almost everything except for two areas, both not coincidentally language related. As part of New Jersey's world language emphasis at the time, the school introduced Spanish right away. Apparently believing that she was going to be forced to drop English and learn a whole new language again, Callan refused to participate during the lessons. She simply would not speak, no matter how much the teacher coaxed her.

The second issue resulted from Callan having learned German so well. While German and English use the same alphabet, some of the letters—such as "s," "v," "w," and "z"—are pronounced differently. When we were told Callan was having difficulty recognizing the sounds these letters made, we were not surprised. She was pronouncing the letters in German rather than English. We were also told that she was having difficulty making some sounds, such as the "th" combination, again not surprising given that in German "th" sounds like the English "t". Even the long "i" can have a variety of sounds in German so that when asked if the "i" in "mice" and "bite" made the same sound, Callan said no.

The county-provided testing service determined these speech issues required intervention. Once a week, a speech-language pathologist visited the school and took Callan to a large van where she worked on correct enunciation. While Roberta and I found this absurd, confident that Callan's pronunciation would return in the same way she had quickly mimicked the East German accent, we played along.

A few months later, Callan was declared free of her "problem." Sadly, around the same time, she would also be cured of her German "problem," forgetting everything she had learned. She and Tara had sometimes still played in German, but this trailed off quickly after our return. We planned to have a German dinner once a week, but Callan preferred we "speak New Jersey." Happy not to be hamstrung by the language, we parents capitulated.

But linguists postulate that once someone learns a foreign language, even if that person forgets it, he or she will be able to acquire another language more easily. Callan can only recall a few words of German—often asking us the meaning of a word she hears or reads—yet her pronunciation remains excellent, and she has recently proven herself a nimble learner of French, which she chose since our schools don't offer German. Like her sister, she also has a gift for mimicking accents. We are hoping that although the language of her past is over a decade old, she will continue to draw on this as she applies it to new situations.

While Roberta and I believed that Callan was young enough to adjust to German life and language, Tara had been our real worry. One Fulbright video discussed how teenagers often found living abroad difficult. Though American teens are mired in peer pressures—both positive and negative—removing them from these social structures can prove even more problematic. And we took Tara out of school in eighth grade, a year when these pressures and hormone surges may be at their highest.

Tara struggled with the adjustment at first, preferring activities such as ice skating with friends at a temporary rink near the mall to sitting around and conversing about topics that could range too far and wide. But during dinner one Saturday evening only a few months into our stay, Tara declared, "I just had the strangest experience. I was walking down the street in a medieval German city speaking German with my German friends after we went to see a movie in German. And I thought about all my friends in the U.S. and how none of them will probably ever do this."

I put down my fork and placed my hands on the table's edge as if to rise: "We can go home now."

"What do you mean?" Tara asked.

"You've figured out that your world is a little bigger than you thought it was. And that's the whole purpose of coming here. Now that you realize it, we can go back to the U.S."

"A little bigger?" Tara said. "You mean a lot bigger! I love this town. I love Erfurt."

Six months later, as we packed to move out of our apartment, I said to Tara, "Guess what? The Lindes said you can stay here if you want and live with them." I was joking, of course, but felt real pangs for my insensitivity when her eyes grew large with hope as she exclaimed, "Really?"

Our worry shifted from Tara's adjustment to Erfurt to how she would reacclimate to life in our rural New Jersey town of 3,000 after living in a German city of 200,000. Tara did find returning to the United States awkward. She couldn't even settle back into life with her old friends. Because she was beginning high school and Woodstown has two sending districts, half her classmates were new to the school and to her. Plus, by the time we arrived back in town, she had missed out on all the high school orientation events and had to start marching band and field hockey late. For the second year in a row, she felt as if she were starting behind everyone else.

From the moment she stepped off the plane at the Philadelphia airport in 2001, Tara was planning her next visit to Germany. She said, "My quest ever since that first year has been to find new ways to go back." Two years later, she would return to live with the Lindes as a junior in high school. That year, however, did not start out well. Though Tara was familiar with the language, the people she would be staying with, and the city, she was for the first time without the comfort provided by family. She even wanted to come home during the first few days, but Roberta instructed her to unpack and stick it out for a bit before deciding, her own version of

Frau Lange waving away parental security. That year turned out to be another tremendous experience for her, allowing her to solidify her knowledge of the language and her love of the people, but again she returned to upheaval.

While Tara was spending that junior year abroad, we were offered the opportunity, via a private sale, to purchase a hundred-year-old Victorian home on an acre of land just a few blocks from the university. Roberta and I had spent two years looking for something nearer to work as Roberta was now also employed full time at the university, but we had stopped, thinking we would try again when Tara graduated. Yet this one-of-a-kind house within walking distance of work changed our minds. And although Tara had found Woodstown too small for her liking upon first returning, when she came back from her junior year abroad, she preferred to spend her senior year with the friends she had known for so long, not wanting to be the new kid in the new town yet again. Since Tara has a late-summer birthday, she didn't get her driver's permit until after she returned from Germany, so every day I got up at five and drove her to the high school, dropped her off, and drove back again—an hour-long commute that ended up where it started. Roberta or I repeated the drive in the afternoon or evening, depending on what activities Tara had going on after school.

But we managed, and Tara went off to college, where she majored in international relations and German and spent another junior year abroad, this time sharing an apartment with an actress in Berlin. Tara also went on to receive her master's in international relations with a focus on European politics and served a summer internship with the American Embassy in Berlin. Tara admits she would not be where she is today had we not gone to Erfurt that first time: "Not only did it help me decide what I wanted to study, but it encapsulated everything I want to do in life." For Tara, that year in Germany was clearly her *Wende*, her personal turning point. "When I write to my German friends," she says, "I tell them that I miss my *echtes Heimatland*," my real homeland.

We landed on a Thursday. I returned to work Monday morning. While in Germany, I had accepted a newly created position to coordinate the first-year writing program. We still needed to hire teachers for the fall semester, which began less than a month after we returned from Germany. A week after a chaotic first few days of classes, I was sitting in my office, door slightly ajar, preparing for my own course, when one of the new hires burst through and shouted, "We're under attack! The whole country is being bombed! Oh my God, you must think I'm crazy, but we're being attacked!"

I did not doubt her. Her astonishment and fear were too real. The two of us rushed to the main lobby where, on a bank of televisions, she, I, and others we did not know watched as just before 10:00 a.m. the south tower of the World Trade Center collapsed, followed half an hour later by the north tower.

As the towers dropped repeatedly, I wanted to turn away. Instead, I continued to stare, hoping that just once something different might happen. No words came forth. Even the language we live within sometimes provides no means to express how we feel. Standing in the shadows of structures that no longer existed, I witnessed the present wending into former times. The dividing line between the life before and the life after had been crossed. We had already been conveyed to that foreign land where they do things differently. I took in a deep breath, knowing that it would be a long time before I could once again exhale.

Afterword
Echoes of a Fallen Wall

In the early hours of a dark morning two days after Christmas 2007, the jet that Roberta, Callan, and I were passengers in touched down on a fog-shrouded runway in Frankfurt. The lights from the terminal were barely visible in the predawn darkness. The fog outside the plane as we rolled along the tarmac matched that inside my head after the overnight flight. The color scheme of the airport—gray and off white, inside and out—stunts the palette of the imagination. I could only hope that color would return sometime during the trip.

After retrieving our bags and making our way through customs, we carted our luggage down an endless hallway to the car rental agency where we had our reservation. As we approached, I regretted my desire for color. The company's signature orange, amplified by backlighting, made my eyes water. The young man behind the counter was unbearably chipper for any hour of the day. But I appreciated him more when he offered us a new Volvo station wagon because the smaller car we had ordered was not available.

The glowing orange behind us, we made our way to the concrete parking structure and our gray station wagon camouflaged against the decking and wall. Gyring down several stories of cement, we began the two-hour drive to Erfurt. The fog gave way to rain as we made our way north on the autobahn in the eight a.m. darkness. The gray exterior of our Volvo with less than thirty kilometers on it quickly lost even that color.

Past my former home of Giessen, the rain stopped and the fog returned. A perfect morning for an escape attempt across a channel of the Spree. Of course we were not escaping anything. There were no more borders within Germany, though somewhere farther on, we crossed the area where the Wall once stood. Soon after the *Wende*, this transition was easily noticed as one moved onto the rougher, poorly constructed roads of the former East. Now, these had been replaced by wider, smoother roadways that were in better shape than many roads in the west.

As we neared Erfurt, the weather cleared. By ten o'clock, we arrived at the Lindes'. We were met by Manuela, Wilfried, and their son, Thomas. Their daughter, Anne-Katrin, and our Tara, who was spending her college year abroad in Berlin and had spent Christmas with the Lindes, were still asleep. To keep us travelers from doing likewise in the warmth of the house, we adults went on the customary walk. The Lindes lived on a hill above the city in an area whose summer homes and huts had been converted into or replaced by year-round houses. As we wandered around the Lindes' neighborhood and into the surrounding Steigerwald, Wilfried filled us with stories of life during GDR times in this area, where he had lived in the house his parents bought when he was a child.

As we passed one house, Wilfried told the story of Herr Fisher, who during GDR times owned Fisher Foto in town. The business did well, but Fisher had a lifelong stutter. Thus, saying the name of his own store became F-F-F-Fisher

F-F-Foto. I imagined him answering the shop phone—assuming he had one—while the person on the other end waited patiently for him to finish. Herr Fisher's neighbor owned a Wartburg, the upscale GDR automobile, with a bad muffler. During those times, one had to order such a part, and it might take months or quite possibly years to arrive. Fisher frequently complained to the neighbor because while she had to be at work by seven, he didn't open his shop until ten. As she drove past his house each morning, her loud muffler would awaken him and he could not get back to sleep. Indeed, it became so regular, Fisher stopped setting his alarm clock.

Eventually, the new muffler arrived and the woman had the car repaired. The next evening, an angry Herr Fisher was back on her doorstep. Because she had not told him she was having the repair done, Fisher had overslept and ended up opening his shop over an hour late. I imagined his stuttering chastisement of the neighbor for not informing him he would need to make alternate arrangements to awaken in the morning.

Farther along, we passed an opening into a field. Wilfried informed us that although he had been stationed in a different town when he was an East German soldier, his unit would bivouac here. While the soldiers took target practice, Wilfried could hear his German shepherd at his parents' house on the other end of the woods barking at the commotion. Often his mother would visit him and, being the caring mother she was, bring schnapps for him and his companions to make their time in the woods a little more tolerable.

Wilfried also pointed out some nearby trees with initials and dates carved into them. He said that when a soldier's release date was imminent, he would often scrawl this reminder to others that someday their military service would end.

I took the opportunity to ask Wilfried about the woods itself. The Lindes heat their home using wood that Wilfried retrieves by cutting up fallen trees. I asked if it is okay to do so. "One can, but it's not allowed," Wilfried told me, hinting at a winking subversiveness that has survived the GDR.

On another afternoon, Roberta and I left Callan with the Lindes and drove into Erfurt's city center, mostly to see how places we had known half a dozen years earlier now looked. But our first stop was a new one for us. Manuela had told us that the Gutenberg Gymnasium had been renovated since the Robert Steinhäuser massacre. The government poured money into refurbishing the building and replacing much of the faculty, removing both the reminders and the rememberers of the shooting. Gutenberg is now among the most desirable high schools in a city where school selection is by choice, not based on home address. The building, I was surprised to find out, stands in the middle of a neighborhood with apartment buildings across the street. The early-twentieth-century Jugendstil style contrasts flowing rooflines, numerous windows, and cream paint with a castlelike solidity defined by turrets and a vaulted entranceway that discourage visitors.

Though a light display announced the school's one-hundredth anniversary, Gutenberg Gymnasium is better known around the world for Steinhäuser's 2002 attack. At the right front of the building, burned candles in jars, a small wreath, and some cigarette butts lay scattered on the ground before a brushed nickel plaque that lists the names of Steinhäuser's sixteen victims and their occupations: a secretary, a police officer, two students who were unintentionally killed when he shot through locked doors, and twelve teachers. From this, Steinhäuser's search image seems clear.

In addition to the main entrance, which sits atop a massive set of stairs that echo those climbing to Mariendom and St. Severus a few blocks away, the original building is also flanked by side doors with mottos carved into the stone above each. On one side the motto read *Lebe um zu Lernen*: Live in order to learn. The other side read *Lerne um zu Leben*: Learn in order to live. As the renovations were planned, I imagine debates must have taken place over whether to keep these mottoes. While each represents hope in the power of education to transform lives, they also demonstrate the bitter irony for those whose lives were cut short while enacting these words.

Later, I examined the information collected by my digital camera. We spent twenty minutes walking around the building, reading the names on the memorial and taking photographs—the same amount of time Steinhäuser's shooting spree is estimated to have lasted.

Before New Year's, Wilfried and Manuela drove us to the Grenzlandmuseum Eichsfeld, a borderland museum. Sever-

al of these dot the landscape where East and West once met. After an hour or so moving through small towns and rolling countryside with rises in the distance, we entered hilly terrain. The roads were narrow, winding. Wilfried put on a CD. Emmylou Harris's plaintive yet soothing voice filled the car. "Hello, Stranger," sang Emmylou as we neared the border, and I realized my flash fiction piece "American, the Beautiful" had a doppelgänger.

During GDR times, such music from the West would have been banned and expensive to obtain on the black market. Wilfried had recently shown us his prized *Schwarzmarkt* purchase, an LP version of—what else— Pink Floyd's *The Wall*, which he acquired shortly after its 1973 release. He paid 100 East German marks for it at a time when 600 East German marks was a month's normal take-home pay. As he stared wistfully at the cover, I wanted to be the listening device inside his head.

The winding roads dropped us down into a valley that

opened into flat land again. Finally, we arrived at the border. Instead of continuing into what had been the West, we turned into the Grenzlandmuseum, where outside sat GDR military vehicles, a helicopter used for border patrol, and even the original guard tower with views of the surrounding countryside. To enter the indoor exhibit, one had to move through a narrow passport control area, where a mannequin dressed in an olive green outfit stretched out his hand, awaiting one's identity papers. We ignored him.

Farther in, the cashier's young son, perhaps five or six, sat next to her and scrutinized us much more than the mannequin had. He narrowed his eyes while we paid our entrance fee and spoke to each other in English. To ingratiate myself, I pulled a dollar bill from my wallet and placed it on the counter him. "Das kommt aus Amerika," I told him. He looked at it and said nothing. "Du kannst es haben." You can have it. He stared at the foreign object for a moment then more closely at us as we wandered away. My feeble attempt at international diplomacy had failed.

Among the GDR artifacts inside—including Stasi listening devices and recording instruments; a prison cell; and dioramas, photographs, and signs from the border area—we came across a *Rollbarer Spiegel der Zollkontrolle*, a wheeled mirror that allowed customs officers at the Wall to inspect for alterations under vehicles. A few months earlier, Roberta, Callan, and I had traveled from our southern New Jersey home to Washington, D.C. We drove around the mall area looking for a parking spot. Finding none, we finally followed some official-looking signs that directed us toward a parking structure.

A block off Constitution Avenue, we were confronted by a booth and a metal barrier. A man in uniform stepped from behind the one-way glass of the small building. He came over to our German-made VW and asked to see photo identification. Roberta and I handed over our licenses. The guard studied these, took a long look at eleven-year-old Callan sitting in the back, and returned the documents to me. He asked me to pop the trunk and poked around among our bags. Then he retrieved a wheeled mirror device and walked around the car, rolling it underneath to see what bomb components we might have hidden in the chassis. Finally, he came back around to the driver's side, took our fee, and told us to have a nice day. He signaled to an unseen colleague in the booth; the barrier disappeared into the ramp.

Staring at the *Rollbarer Spiegel der Zollkontrolle* here at the border museum, I was amazed both at the similarity of the devices and how we in America, when visiting the Ronald Reagan Building, can now feel as if we are living in the GDR. The only difference appears to be in whether it is those attempting to get in or those trying to get out who are the target of the search.

The similarities do not end there. In the United States, some believe it is acceptable to imprison people for years without charging them with a crime. Some believe it is government's right to listen in on conversations without just cause. Some believe that building a fence will solve the problems attributed to bordering states. Some are choosing security over liberty. As I make these claims I imagine how these might provide my e-mail correspondents—the ones who thought I was making accusatory and inflammatory remarks when I wrote that Robert Steinhäuser borrowed western ideas—something new to seethe over. But, they might very well argue, our situation in the United States is different. I might even agree. Perhaps our problems are different. But our solutions have come to resemble one another.

Roberta and I caught a streetcar out to our old *Plattenbau* neighborhood. With the car mostly to ourselves, I took photos of Roberta perfecting what we refer to as the *Strassenbahn* stare, the look of ennui often seen on riders for whom this is their regular transportation.

Much looked the same during the eighteen-minute ride. The old city, comprised of buildings with shops below and apartments above, gave way to the newer and sometimes detached housing with a few big box stores interspersed. The university slid by. We did not get off, though the University's gates had been removed. At the stop in front of Thüringen-Park mall, we disembarked into a drizzle and clutched each other as we crossed Moskauerstrasse and headed into the *Plattenbau* labyrinth.

The renovation of the three buildings facing the tracks —each eleven stories high and more than a city block long—had been completed in our absence. Starting with firebrick red on the main floor, each row of balconies moved

through a muted version of a rainbow: mauve, orange, tangerine, yellow. But the top floor balconies were painted white, as if the designer had run out of ideas or the contractor out of pigment. In the dreariness of the day, the tops of the buildings blended into the sky.

We walked toward our former home, the few people we encountered hunching against the rain. As we rounded the corner, I spied the parking spot from which our Escort had been escorted. Nearby, blocks from the wall that once surrounded our playground had toppled or been pushed to the ground. I doubt there was a celebration over this now-crumbled wall.

Beyond this stood our unremodeled building. On closer inspection, the balconies were all empty, the windows without curtains. Abandoned. We followed the path of ground-floor graffiti—as colorful as the balconies and painted as high as a person can reasonably reach—to the front of the building. The entryway was gated off with a metal door, already rusting. Above, our and Tara's bedroom windows had been broken by rocks. Two gaping holes of jagged glass looked out on the concrete courtyard.

We kept walking deeper into the neighborhood. More *Plattenbau* had been remodeled: one with a bright rainbow effect, another in blue-gray and red. We passed Callan's former kindergarten. A sign in the window indicated the names of the teachers. Only two were left, neither of them our treasured Frau Lange.

We rounded a corner to confront our own building's future. A *Plattenbau* had been dismantled and neatly stacked like dirty gray dishes on a counter. This was not surprising given the decreasing population, the housing being built or renovated, and that the once-desirable amenities of central heat and bathrooms no longer attracted newcomers to Erfurt's outskirts. A backhoe's crooked yellow arm waved from behind the pile. It continued to rain. We walked on, passing another demolition site. More stacked plates.

We returned to the *Strassenbahn* stop and awaited its arrival. Soon, the lighted red streetcar came into view and stopped before us. The new southward destination point for the Number 3 line had been lengthened to Urbicher Kreuz. We entered, escaping the rain, the pending darkness, and for the last time the neighborhood we once called home. We knew we didn't need to visit this area again where our former lives would soon lay crushed between ceiling and floor. Had I found a stone to toss through my old bedroom window, I would have done so, too.

On the last day of 2007, we left Erfurt for Berlin. Tara was spending her third year in Germany, this time studying at Humboldt-Universität in what was once East Berlin. Tara seemed to have adopted her deep affection for foreign countries from Roberta's mother, Karin, the Augsburg native who has passed her half-century mark living in the United States. In a recent letter, Karin closed with a reference to Tara: "She seems to love it there, like I love to be in America, and still do. As long as I can remember I was fascinated with America. I always wished my family would emigrate when I was in grade school. Once the teacher asked us what we would like to do when we grow up. I said I want to go and live in America, and I never regretted it." And now Tara has adopted her *oma*'s homeland as her own. She can even fool native speakers into believing she is from there. While being interviewed at a Berlin bar where she was watching the Super Bowl in the middle of the night, the TV reporter, assuming she was German even after talking with her, wondered why Tara knew so much about the game and the teams playing. Tara had to explain that as an American she had sat through many a Super Bowl party.

Even though Tara spent Christmas with the Lindes and so was with us in Erfurt, we wanted to visit Berlin again, to see the city from Tara's perspective so that when she wrote and talked about it and sent us pictures, we would have a better idea of *her* Berlin.

Tara lived in the former East, a block from Bernauerstrasse, where the Wall had once split East and West. However, the West laid claim to the actual road, so when the Wall was first constructed, the sidewalk outside the East German apartments was in another country. This led to people first jumping from the buildings' windows to escape, some fatally injuring themselves while doing so, and then digging tunnels under the road once the inhabitants of the apartments were removed by the state.

Tara rented a room in the apartment of Ilka Teichmüller, an actress who grew up in the GDR. The Wall fell while Ilka was studying acting at the famous Babelsberg studios in

Potsdam, where Fritz Lang's *Metropolis* and von Sternberg's *The Blue Angel*, featuring Marlene Dietrich, were made.

Ilka told me over martinis that after the Wall fell, she put in a request to see her Stasi file. "I was so disappointed to find out there was nothing in it. My mother, too. Just one letter from my aunt in the U.S. We are so boring," she lamented.

We were sitting in the appropriately named Bar Roberta, a streetfront *Kneipe* with high stools, wooden tables, and sconces that cast a yellow light over the large room. I asked Ilka about her father, who had recently passed away. "I don't think he asked to see his file," she responded without explanation.

Our conversation turned to how Ilka, who was "eighteen or nineteen" when the Wall fell, learned to adjust to the free-market system. Prior to this, the concept of capitalism was not new to her. She was introduced to it in school long before the *Wende*: "We were told about how capitalism worked. We were told about the evil system that created capitalism, but not that capitalism itself was evil. It has turned out to be everything we were told it was."

In GDR times, Ilka continued, "Everyone understood the rules, and then there could be some Till Eulenspiegel." She made this last reference because she knew I would understand it. Till Eulenspiegel, a trickster character from folklore, is a symbol adopted by Erfurt and is also the name of our cat, acquired when we returned to the United States after our yearlong stay. To "do some Till Eulenspiegel" is to overturn the rules, to invert the normal hierarchies. While this is common in celebrations such as Mardi Gras, Carnival, and Fasching, in East Germany such Till Eulenspiegel would have been more covert, occurring beyond the watchful eyes of the state.

"With capitalism," she added, "one doesn't know the rules."

This lack of certitude created by capitalism affected Ilka immediately. The three-year acting contract she would have been guaranteed at the end of her studies never materialized. Now, she freelances, hustling for each acting job, her future never planned out more than a few months in advance.

"Where I studied," Ilka went on, "the cafeteria was on the second floor and had a big balcony. We could look over the Wall and into the West while eating our lunches."

But such a position did not entice her to think of escape. "As a teen in Weimar," Ilka said, referring to her hometown where Roberta had been rebuffed for her search of a simple memento, "I worked as a tour guide for Westerners." One woman from the United States introduced her to Velvet Underground's "After Hours," a song performed by drummer Maureen Tucker, with its refrain that almost too easily applies to the GDR and life behind the Wall:

All the people are dancing
and they're having such fun
I wish it could happen to me.

After the Wall came down, Ilka visited America and the song-sharing friend: "We were driving through the deserts of the western United States and the song came on the CD. I broke down and cried because, as a girl helping these people and hearing this song, I never had any idea that I might be here. I never imagined it. There was no chance for it to happen, so why would I think it might be possible?"

We spent New Year's 2008 as part of Deutschlands Grösste Party Meile, Germany's Biggest Party Mile, at the Brandenburg Gate, a scene of revelry, drinking, and fireworks that surely rivaled celebrations when the Wall fell. Perhaps it even provided a hint of what it must have been like to live in an area under siege. Blasts and sprays of sparks flew everywhere. Smoke drifted through the night sky. People filled the streets, shouting and gasping. Vacant eyes stared at the fireworks. Yet marauders did not cause this mayhem; rather, the constant turmoil was the result of New Year's revelers who began their fireworks and public displays of mass drunkenness long before midnight. Between 6:00 p.m. on New Year's Eve and 6:00 a.m. on New Year's Day, Berlin fire companies would respond to almost 1,700 calls, police to nearly 1,800. At the Brandenburg Gate party, over 250 people were treated for injuries or illness due to overconsumption. These figures were actually down from previous years.

In walking to and from the party, we passed dozens of groups holding their own private street celebrations and shooting off fireworks. Callan, who does not like loud noises, walked with her mittened hands over her ears, making her a target for those who entertained themselves by tossing firecrackers at the feet of passersby. Later, we came across a scene that typified the excesses of the night. A man sat in an entryway, back against the wall. He listed, leaning on an elbow. His legs were akimbo, a large puddle of vomit near and on one of them. Two police officers, standing judiciously out of projectile range, were trying to convince the man he needed to leave. Whether the man knew how to get home was debatable; his inability to get himself there was not.

It seemed appropriate that with such self-destructive tendencies, we overheard many people on New Year's speaking of having *überlebt*—survived—the year. Though the lack of optimism in this declaration surprised me, it should not have. The New Year's celebration—called *Silvester* in German—parallels the fall of the Wall. What started out as a huge party filled with hopes for better times has ended up with many people grateful to have survived. Ilka had spoken to me of such circumstances: "I have friends who think that if someone is poor or in a bad situation, it's their responsibility. Part of it might be, but you need both the free market and a strong social structure."

"Those friends make me so angry when they talk like this," she added.

Or perhaps this overexuberance is just a little of the Till Eulenspiegel coming out in people, the evening and crowds permitting everyone a chance to play the fool.

I had been sitting on the toilet lid in a Berlin hotel bathroom for more than an hour. It was just after 6:00 a.m. on New Year's Day. On the east coast of the United States, our friends had recently rung in the new year. Roberta tapped on the bathroom door. I looked up from my words scrawled across white paper. The walls, floor, fixtures and towels were all white. A long mirror and glass partition in the tub reemphasized the starkness.

I got up and opened the door.

Roberta squinted against the suddenness of light. "Are you all right?" she whispered.

"I'm fine," I assured her. I had been writing, my notebook resting on a small stool before me.

I awoke from my brief New Year's slumber to the realization that I was sleeping in a metaphor. Still in the clutches of the beer and champagne we had consumed, I did not want to forget this thought. I had felt around in the dark for my notebook then taken it into the bathroom, hoping not to awaken anyone.

This was our first visit to Berlin since 2000, when the four of us attended the Fulbright orientation. Our fifteenth-story hotel room that overlooked Alexanderplatz and its landmark TV tower was located in the Forum (which rhymes with "kaboom" when pronounced in German), once the GDR's preeminent hotel, though it was called the Hotel Stadt Berlin then. The rooms were small and not air-conditioned. Even in 2000, the furnishings consisted of plain gray veneer, and the carpeting was similarly slate gray. Tourism in Berlin had skyrocketed over the past few years, which translated into a shortage of hotel rooms. Thus, such a room in the Forum (which has since been renamed the more westernized Park Inn) normally went for $150 a night, although a nice apartment in eastern Berlin could be had for $500 a month because so many easterners were moving to the west, leaving behind their empty living spaces.

I wondered if East Germans had used the Forum as a honeymoon spot and, if so, how that would work out, since each room held two single beds situated at 45-degree angles to one another. As in Regensburg, Roberta and I had pushed ours together into a makeshift double, albeit with a chasm down the middle. We were surprised when we returned the next afternoon to find that our beds had been made by housekeeping, but that they had been left where they were. Surely, we presumed, those overly efficient, rule-bound Germans would not allow us to break the conventions of proper bed placement.

Or perhaps they were just accommodating the future. During that 2000 stay, the Forum's upper floors were under renovation to make them more appealing to westerners. This included adding air-conditioning, modem connections, safes, and what the ads called "French-style beds," though we Americans refer to these simply as double beds.

I have yet to see an actual double bed in a German hotel or home. The German equivalent is what Roberta and I constructed: two single beds pushed together but outfitted with separate sheets and comforters. This *Doppelbett* is as customary in Germany as separate pillows are anywhere else.

The thought of these divided hotel double beds as metaphor had jarred me out of my first, short sleep of the new year. When the Wall stood, Berliners shared a *Doppelbett* within the larger *Doppelbett* of Germany. A *Doppelbett* with the split down the middle—that black gash on the landscape in the news stories I watched as a kid—was so much like the two Berlins and like the two Germanys. Simultaneously alone and together. Desirous and disdainful of one another. Cleaving in both senses of the word: adhering and splitting apart.

Prior to the construction of the Wall, Easterners were allowed to travel and even work in the West. The division of Berlin into sectors was, in the eyes of the people, a figment of the state's imagination. But in 1961 the East German government had decided this arrangement allowed too much intimacy, too much contact with the West. As Lutz Rathenow says in *Ost-Berlin*, "Fencing off is only viewed as necessary when things threaten to intermingle." In erecting the Wall, the GDR attempted to replace the double bed with a *Doppelbett*. But doing so separated families, lovers and those who simply desired to be on the other side. As with two who are attracted to each other sharing a bed, action eventually becomes irrepressible. Many attempted to escape, crossing over the *Doppelbett* gap. That Germans were living in this *Doppelbett* became tangible any time someone tried to cross the Wall, any time a banned item was smuggled from one land to the other, any time radio or television waves traveled to the other side. This passing across was an illicit sexual escapade, a prohibited foray. But the fissure that was the Wall could not thwart desire.

On the New Year's morning that I wrote in the Berlin bathroom of the Home Suite Home hotel, I finally tired and retreated from my metaphoric to my actual bed, a real *Doppelbett* with its separate mattresses, sheets and comforters. No sunlight had begun to penetrate the heavy curtains as I placed my notebook onto the bedside stand and slid under the sheets. A police car wailed down the street, as they had all night long. I lived for a few minutes within the words of Rathenow, who says, "Early New Year's morning, I was awakened over and over again by the sound of sirens. Berlin is not a place for sleeping." I reached over and found Roberta, who hadn't read Rathenow, asleep on her side of the bed. I tried to cross the divide. I sprawled my body over it, a hand on her back and a leg against hers. I awaited sleep. Nothing. I curled against Roberta, an arm around her. Waited some more. Still nothing.

As we lay in a bed once located in East Berlin, situated halfway between the one-time ghost station of Nordbahnhof and the border crossing on Invalidenstrasse, the morning light pushed against the other side of the windows, seeping through cracks in the drapes. The past of night became the present of day. One cannot sleep astride a wall.

Since our last visit to Berlin, the DDR (Deutsche Demokratische Republik) Museum had opened. Roberta read aloud from the website: "Experience history in a vivid, interactive and playful way: The DDR Museum offers you a hands-on experience of the everyday life of a state long gone, the life in socialism. Visitors are welcome to . . . reconsider existing clichés and to have a hands-on experience of history . . . Everything waits to be touched and experienced:

Open the drawers and closets, rummage through them and discover!"

"Why would we want to see that?" Roberta mock-scoffed.

"We lived it."

There is an irony in saying this. We often ask Manuela and Wilfried about life in GDR times. They willingly share stories or take us to places like the border museums Roberta and I so love to visit, but they must wonder, why the interest, why the fascination? Why are these Americans so gripped by a time they never lived through?

I imagine that those who escaped the GDR would, as soon as they felt safe, take a look back. As with Brian Rose's photograph of the Wall, I believe that they would want to see, out of curiosity, what the other side of the Wall, the side they had never seen, looked like and also, out of a sense of security, reassure themselves that now they were indeed on that side. So too do we need to look back, to resee what we know from a different position. Thus, we couldn't miss a chance to visit the DDR Museum. We wanted to experience "the everyday life of a state long gone" because, just as the first time we lived it, we had the choice to do so. We had not been forced to live this life; we had not feared that our every move might be watched and chronicled, to be used against us at a later date. Nor did we fear, as with Lot's wife, that we would be turned into a pillar of salt, forever petrified for looking back. Indeed, we continue to seek out this time period because each encounter reveals more, making us less firm in the positions we take for granted. Visiting the museum would allow us to compare some official—if playful—version of the GDR to the stories the Lindes have told and to the transitional version of the GDR we lived in for a year.

So on New Year's Day, that time of new beginnings, we found ourselves rummaging around inside a building on the

Spree riverfront, the water passage to freedom that the elder Lindes and young Wilfried did not cross. I tucked myself into a Trabant for the first time. Tara climbed into the passenger seat. We marveled at the crude simplicity of the dash instrumentation and the hole for a glove box. True to its reputation, the fickle Trabi did not start when I turned the key, though it did for Callan when she took her turn. She drove it through a videotaped *Plattenbau* district—what the placard referred to as a "concrete-slab housing estate"—displayed on a screen in front of the car. This might have been where we had lived, except that the fashions of pedestrians were clearly pre-*Wende* and, instead of seeing an occasional Trabi, as was the case in our neighborhood in 2000–2001, the street and parking spots were filled with them.

We learned for the first time about the proclivity for nude beaches in GDR times. A six-foot-long diorama with over two dozen six-inch-high nude figurines revealed this in three dimensions. Some sunbathed, others played volleyball, a group swam, one rubbed oil on the back of another, and the figure nearest the front of the scene stood before a sign saying "nude sunbathing area begins here." Already topless, she was in the midst of pulling off her bathing suit bottom, mooning viewers on the other side of the glass. Till Eulenspiegel.

While visiting the living room of the completely restored GDR-style apartment, Callan and I picked up a deck of tattered cards and played a game of Crazy Eights. I felt as if I were at home in Erfurt again. Most who walked past ignored us. They milled about, pulling the chain to flush the toilet, complete with sound effects, and snooped through cupboards in the kitchen or the cabinets in the living room. Others stopped and watched our game for a few moments, as if we were part of the exhibit. We did not learn, until revisiting the website later, of the listening device hidden behind a picture above where we had been sitting and chatting.

We decided to stop in Berlin Story, a souvenir shop along Unter den Linden, a former East German street with the Brandenburg Gate at one end and Humboldt University at the other. *Linden* is the plural of *Linde*, which means "lime tree" and is also Wilfried and Manuela's last name. A double-rowed grove of these trees line the central mall. I squinted as I moved from the darkness of late afternoon to the brightly lit store's interior. Roberta, Tara, Callan, and I headed our separate ways, studying the books, the T-shirts, the East and West German kitsch. What has capitalism decided represents the essence of the Wall, of Berlin, of Germany? What part of the experience do people want to take home with them? What artifacts will remind them of their excursion?

I passed a large section of *Ampelmännchen* paraphernalia. The green and red traffic signal men stood on and walked across sponges, towels, umbrellas, pasta, flower holders, lamps, snow domes, corkscrews, ice cube trays, cookie cutters, postcards, key chains, coffee mugs, T-shirts, even lychee-flavored (red) and peppermint-flavored (green) vodka. Capitalist green from communist red.

Farther down the row, I came across several shelves holding busts of famous Germans. There among Prussian icons Queen Louise, Kaiser Wilhelm, and Frederick the Great, I spied an identifiable high hairline and large beard. Not only did they carry the standard gypsum white model but also one in red rusted iron, the latter an exclusive to this store, according to the sign. These two rows of red and white Karl Marx stood at eye level. His deep-set eyes stared past me, over my right shoulder.

I called to Roberta, who joined me.

Karl Marx
aus Gips
17.50 €

Exklusiv für die Berlin Story
Karl Marx

"It's Marx! Do you want one?"

She looked them over, never took her hands from her jacket pockets.

"No thanks," she replied.

"Really? You were searching for one for so long. We could make sure to pack him carefully. He'll survive the trip."

"No. That time has passed," she said. "Those are former times."

Visiting the Jewish Museum Berlin is frustrating. Intentionally so. Architect Daniel Libeskind places the visitor within a space that undermines expectations of what a museum should be and do. This structure—for to call it a building pushes that word to the limits of expectation—is different from other museums, most of which intend to provide an aesthetically pleasing display area for the contents. Libeskind's edifice attempts to confound, isolate, and disconcert.

The Jewish Museum Berlin is really two buildings: a baroque Old Building—once home to the Prussian supreme court—and Libeskind's New Building, whose layout seems based on a pencil's zigzagging path through a maze. Although the zinc-clad exterior and largely concrete interior are comprised of lines, few form right angles. Sightlines are truncated, and each turn presents the unexpected. A funhouse without the whimsy.

The symmetrical Old Building has become an injured bird, the red roof its underbelly revealed to the sky. Libeskind's contorted structure is its broken wing, the few windows the predator's gashes. As if the attacker had amputated it in the struggle, the twisted wing no longer attaches to the bird itself, separated by several yards from the Old Building. And yet Libeskind's creation somehow flies, albeit on a jagged, jolting, and erratic path.

As so often happens with such disfigurement, the wound becomes the attraction. The sabotaging of expectations begins immediately. One enters through the Old Building but must go downstairs to enter the New. Once in the extension, the visitor encounters three "axes": Continuity, Exile, and the Holocaust. The Axis of the Holocaust's sloping floors and inclining walls lead to an empty silo with no heating or cooling and only a small slit of natural light coming through an opening at the top, some three floors up. The Axis of Exile leads to an outside garden that unbalances a visitor with its thick, inclined pillars and tilted foundation. The hallways of these two axes contain some personal belongings. The mundane photos are powerful only because we know the outcome of those photographed following these innocent moments. The kids' drawings, normally filled with their own innocence, here illustrate the consequences of Diaspora and Holocaust. The Axis of Continuity leads to the main galleries. First, though, one must climb three flights of squeeze-to-get-by stairs, which appear to lead nowhere, ending in a wall. It is only when one nears the top that the entrance to the exhibits reveals itself.

As I moved from one display to another throughout the building, I was struck by how uncomfortably they sit within the building itself. The goal of the Jewish Museum Berlin is to cover the two-thousand-year history of Jews in Germany. In attempting to normalize the Jewish experience, these exhibits are at odds with Libeskind's design. Libeskind wishes to make the building itself the experience. Many agree. After the New Building was completed in 1999 but before any exhibits were installed two years later, 350,000 people visited the empty annex. And while Mirjam Wenzel, head of the museum's media department, claims that the Holocaust cannot be represented, Libeskind asks the visitor to sense, in at least some small way, the disorientation and displacement that characterizes Jewish history.

My lingering recollection will always be that of "Fallen Leaves," an installation in one of the six memory voids Libeskind has placed throughout the wing. The only void that can be entered, "Fallen Leaves" resides within a narrow space whose concrete walls, like that of the Holocaust void, reach skyward several stories. Entering the dimly lit interior, I was struck by the loudness. Clanging echoed throughout the concrete tower. I could sense movement, others walking across the room somehow causing the noise. As my eyes adjusted, I saw thousands of plate-sized film reels spread across the floor, each with an open-mouthed face reminiscent of Munch's *The Scream*. These are made of iron, and with each step, the fallen leaves clank together, sending forth the reverberating clatter.

As impressed as I was with what Libeskind had created, I was equally awed by his having completed, as he says in the video *Le musée juif de Berlin* (part of the *Architectures 3* series on the European public TV channel ARTE), "a space that really actually never existed" prior to this. I have spent years working on this book. I have been hindered by not allowing that shadows from fallen walls, like all shadows, shift and take on new shapes as the sun hits at different angles. So too will my perspective keep shifting; it will continue to be altered by the moving arc of time. Libeskind's structural phenomenon, necessitating a journey in disorientation echoing my own travels in this book, gives me permission to complete my own project even though it, like his New Building, "will always remain something that subverts any attempt to control, make the story finite, and finish with it."

I had only been off the airplane a few minutes when I made my first mistake on the trip. In the early morning ashen gray of the Frankfurt airport, I stopped at a newsstand to pick up a copy of the *International Herald Tribune*. When I went to pay for the paper, I held out my hand to receive the change. The woman ignored my open palm and dropped the money into a tray between us. In Germany, the customer is then to pick the coins out of the tray, a divide across which such exchanges are conducted. By trying to take the coins directly from her I had revealed that I was not German. I reinforced this by placing the coins into my pants pocket. In Germany, men's wallets contain a small, snap-closing compartment to hold change. If the clerk had any doubt of my not being German, this provided her assurance that I wasn't.

We also learned during this trip that we had long been making a German social blunder. With every new round of drinks, one toasts, usually by saying *Prost!* or *Zum Wohl!* This we knew. But Tara relayed that Ilka had pointed out that during the requisite clinking of glasses the two people whose glasses are touching should look into each other's eyes. We were shocked not to have known this. How many times had we said *Prost!* or *Zum Wohl!*—not just on this trip but during all our time in Germany—and not looked into the eyes of those whom we were with? We must have insulted dozens of people. On our day-before-New-Year's celebration with Wilfried and Manuela before leaving Erfurt, we had toasted with Rotkäppchen—a sparkling wine that is one of several East German products that has *überlebt* the Wall's fall. Had we not looked them in the eyes while raising our glasses high? Roberta and I quickly adopted this convention and, over the many vacation beers to follow, we made eye contact, perhaps for slightly longer than we needed. We like this new tradition because it reminds us how much we enjoy the company of the person we are sharing our drink with.

My last mistake of the trip occurred again in the Frankfurt airport, this time on our way back to the United States. Once more, it was early morning. Again I was tired, having awoken early to catch a flight from Berlin to Frankfurt. We walked into the Passport Control area with its unappealing stalls, the opposite of kissing booths, where the humorless workers begin staring at you long before you reach the counter. As the Passport Control officer in a green sweater and white shirt extended his hand in anticipation of the soon-to-be surrendered passport, his robotic movement reminded me of the green-uniformed mannequin in the glass-partitioned booth at the Grenzlandmuseum a few days earlier. The demeanor required of this position is not confined to any country or time period.

He asked us how long we had been in Germany.

"Nine days," I responded.

He shuffled through my passport and came across my 2000–2001 work visa pasted near the back.

"Sprechen Sie Deutsch?" he asked.

In the short flight from Berlin to Frankfurt, I had mentally shifted away from my semi-German mode of thinking and back into English. I didn't want to shift back again.

"Ja, ein bisschen," I responded. A little.

"Leben Sie noch in Deutschland?" Do you still live in Germany, he asked, but I heard this as being in the past tense for some reason: Did you already live in Germany?

"Ja," I said.

"Nein," Roberta immediately spoke up.

I realized my mistake and chimed in, "In zwei tausend." In 2000. Then I stupidly added, "Noch nicht," not yet, when I meant "nicht mehr," no longer.

I was sure this made no sense to the man, who politely ignored me and handed back our passports, dismissing us with a sweep of his hand. And though this was not what I intended to say, it was emblematic of my times in Germany—mistake-filled and often out of context, trying but failing, limited in ways I am not in my native culture.

Walking through the door of our New Jersey home, Roberta quips, "We've escaped from the GDR again." We pour ourselves beers, look into each other's eyes, and say "*Prost!*" Later, we crawl into our double bed without the fissure down the middle. After Roberta falls asleep, I run my finger along her spine then spoon against her back, no longer traversing a divide or straddling a wall. I am instead—as Manuela astutely declared in her e-mail after the Gutenberg school shooting—at once on both sides, insider and outsider to a land that I am *no longer* and *not yet* living in.